REAL SOLUTIONS for Abuse-Proofing Your Child

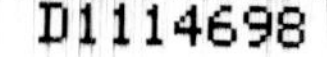

REAL SOLUTIONS for Abuse-Proofing Your Child

Grace Ketterman

SERVANT PUBLICATIONS
ANN ARBOR, MICHIGAN

Vine Books is an imprint of Servant Publications especially designed to serve evangelical Christians.

While the stories in this book are based on real events, they are composites. All the names and identifying details have been changed to protect the identities of the people involved.

Published by Servant Publications
P.O. Box 8617
Ann Arbor, Michigan 48107

Cover design by David Uttley Design

01 02 03 04 10 9 8 7 6 5 4 3 2 1

Printed in the United States of America
ISBN 1-56955-246-0

Library of Congress Cataloging-in-Publication Data

Ketterman, Grace H.
Real solutions for abuse-proofing your child / Grace Ketterman.
p. cm.
Includes bibliographical references.
ISBN 1-56955-246-0 (alk. paper)
1. Child abuse—Prevention. I. Title.

HV6626.5 .K48 2001
649'.4—dc21

2001022235

Contents

1

Recognizing Child Abuse

During the years of my residency in pediatrics, I worked with a child whom I have never forgotten. Jane was eighteen months old and weighed barely twelve pounds. She lay like a little wax doll in her hospital crib, hardly moving, her expression blank. She would take only a bottle and refused all other foods.

I was certain at first that this child had severe neurological impairment, but all the available tests proved otherwise. Her behavior baffled everyone, especially me, until we received the report from our social worker. She had learned that Jane's mother was seriously mentally ill, and though she loved her baby, was unable to care for her beyond the most meager feeding and bathing.

What a challenge!

To counteract Jane's early neglect, we found a loving volunteer grandmother who spent many hours daily with the little girl. This kind woman tickled Jane, rocked her, sang to her, and moved her tiny, weak arms and legs until the muscles regained their function. As the days passed we saw this waxen doll become a real, live child who responded to us, smiled, giggled, cooed, and crawled.

Neglect as severe as that Jane suffered is rare, but her condition when I first examined her reflects the damage that can be done when a child is abused. Child abuse, defined as any treatment of a child that threatens his or her safety and leaves lifelong physical or emotional scars,[1] has existed since the beginning of humankind. It occurs all over the world and varies in type and extent, depending on factors including social mores, family dynamics, and a child's inborn temperament.

Sadly, child abuse appears to be on the rise. In 1990, there were 801,143 cases of verified child abuse. By 1993, that figure had increased to 1,057,255 substantiated cases.[2] In 1998, Wang and Daro discovered that about 47 out of every 1,000 children are reported to be victims of child maltreatment. From 1985 to 1996, they report, the rate of child abuse fatalities increased by 34 percent.[3] The reports included physical abuse, sexual abuse, neglect, and emotional maltreatment. More abuse victims were female than male, but the numbers of reported cases increased similarly for both genders. Abused children ranged in age from less than one year to eighteen years and over, although the highest numbers were in the two- to five-year bracket, and abuse dropped off substantially after age eighteen.

In the United States we regularly read about child abuse—physical, sexual, emotional, and spiritual. Abuse happens in both poor and rich families. It is perpetrated by both strangers and intimates. And it happens in places where people feel safe—at home, at school, at church. Hidden cameras reveal abuse by seemingly competent baby-sitters in the child's own home. School policies and the staff members who carry them out can be tragically abusive in the guise of trying to motivate students. The same is true of methods used by coaches to try to motivate young athletes. Children even abuse each other. No matter its source, abuse always inflicts great pain, both physical and emotional, on its victims.

Now for the good news: You as a parent can proactively abuse-proof your children. In fact, giving your children the skills they need to protect themselves from danger is arguably the most important task you will ever perform as a parent.

Proactive parents are not likely to abuse or neglect their children. They understand why their child misbehaves and they know how to correct their child's mistakes in a loving and effective manner. They understand that childish misbehavior often comes from the pain of unmet needs. They dig until they identify their child's needs—and then they do their best to satisfy those needs.

We'll begin by taking an in-depth look at the many types of child abuse. If you happen to find parts of your own life experience described in these pages, don't be dismayed. Any wounds you've suffered can be healed—and any you've inflicted can be forgiven.

What Does Abuse Look Like?

In order to abuse-proof your children, you must understand exactly what constitutes abuse. As you read about physical, sexual, and emotional abuse, including abuse from neglect and emotional incest, take stock of yourself as a parent. It is just possible that without even realizing it, you may be guilty of one or more of these forms of abuse.

Physical Abuse

I met seven-year-old Shari because her teachers were concerned about changes they had observed in her. Her sparkling blue eyes had become dull and her facial expression sad. Her once shining blonde hair was unkempt and had lost its usual gloss. And even on warm spring days she wore long-sleeved clothing.

When I patted Shari's arm, she grimaced in pain. At my request, she reluctantly pulled up her sleeves. Small, round sores in varying stages of healing covered her thin arms. Several sores were blistered, and a few were covered with drying scabs.

I had seen every sort of trauma in my years of medical practice, but I can recall only a few as heartbreaking as this one. As I gently prodded, Shari began to talk in a terrified whisper. Her voice was so low I had to place my ear close to her mouth to hear her. She told me that her dad drank a lot, and often when he was drunk, he would press a lighted cigarette into her tender flesh, telling her that she had been "bad," and he was punishing her. When I asked Shari how she'd misbehaved, she clearly had no idea. "I think Daddy is trying to teach me to be brave," she whispered.

When confronted, Shari's father insisted that he loved his daughter and was only trying to teach her respect and obedience. Shari's mother, herself terrified of her husband's anger and cruelty, could not find the strength to protect this helpless child. As a result, Shari's world became a jumbled mass of pain and confusion. Just as the marks on her body verified her physical abuse, her sadness, silence, and growing withdrawal wordlessly testified to the damage it was doing to her soul.

Shari's case, though severe, is certainly not isolated. Emergency room staff all too frequently treat children who have been so severely physically abused that their health is threatened and their lives endangered. When questioned, parents reveal that the abuse occurred under the guise of punishing or correcting a wayward child. Tragically, these parents have abandoned one of their most profoundly important roles—protecting their helpless children.

I certainly believe in the need to discipline and correct a child. Occasional, careful swats may be healthy and helpful, but it's never okay to hit a child so hard that the blow raises welts or leaves bruises. When a parent hits, bites, shakes, burns, or scalds a child, that parent is physically abusing the child. Such treatment can have results as serious as broken bones, ruptured internal organs, and brain damage.

The line between discipline and physical abuse can be faint, and tired or overstressed parents may easily cross over it. So may parents who drink too much, who abuse drugs, or who have never learned to recognize their breaking point. Don't take such a chance! There are more healthy ways to correct a child's behavior than physical punishment. (For ideas, see chapter 4.)

Sexual Abuse

Terrence's nightmare began one night when he was eleven, when he awoke in his bed to find his father touching his genitals. He had no idea what to do, so he scooted as far away from the soft, groping hands as he could. But they followed and found him, creating sensations he'd never known. Terrence had no idea what to do with either those feelings or his father.

This cruel invasion continued night after night, contaminating Terrence's soul and convincing him that he was abnormal, dirty, and most of all horribly guilty. He desperately tried to act "normal." He learned to flirt with girls, yet nothing stopped the whisper in his soul that told him he was hopelessly homosexual.

Ashamed of himself and unable to talk with anyone about his relationship with his father, Terrence married a beautiful young woman, but the marriage lasted less than a year. Broken-hearted, lonely, and hopeless, he frantically embraced the gay lifestyle in his community.

When he came to see me, Terrence told me he had the names and addresses of one thousand homosexual partners with whom he had slept. The superficiality and temporary nature of these relationships sickened him. With God's help and intense counseling, this young man finally, miraculously, found redemption and healing, but the scars remain and even now have the capability to cause him distress.

Sexual abuse robs children of their innocence and destroys their trust. When repeated, especially by a family member, it creates ambivalence and indescribable confusion. The excitement of the sexual act, even in children, can make the victim subtly want and yield to more events. But the guilt, helplessness, and fear create a nightmare that at the same time torments them.

When sexual abuse is a recurrent event and becomes mutually consenting, its results can be far-reaching, leaving emotional scars that deform adult life. Children who experience abuse from a parent are especially at risk. When a mother or father becomes a child's sexual partner—at worst, a monster whose size, threats, and abuse are pure torture—the child, in effect, loses that parent as a loving, protective caretaker.

Many victims of sexual abuse in turn victimize others. Abused children frequently molest other children, often a sibling or playmate. They become preoccupied with the secrecy and intensity of the physical stimulation. Girls who are precociously awakened to sexual feelings and become overly focused on them may suffer from nymphomania when they are women. Boys may become addicted to sex in a variety of ways. Abuse becomes a vicious cycle that perpetuates itself and leaves both physical and emotional havoc in its wake. This was true for Elbert.

Many people mistakenly believe that most victims of sexual abuse are girls. In actuality, about one in six boys is sexually abused by the age of sixteen.[4] Elbert was one of them. As a child, he had been molested by his sister, and when I met him he was in prison for sexually molesting his preschool-aged niece. He was still convinced that the little girl really had asked for and enjoyed the sexual contact because she would do little dances and gymnastics in front of him and her family.

Much research has been done around sexual abuse, and a huge bibliography exists on the topic. Equally huge is the range of statistics about its validity. A great many cases are probably never reported, and so the abuse goes on. Unfortunately, when abuse is reported, families are often ripped apart in the aftermath, resulting in yet another abusive event for the child.

Definitions of sexual abuse vary among researchers. Some define it only as aggressive sexual acts with an unwilling victim; others argue that seductive looks and suggestive talk are abusive. In any case, such behavior is always inappropriate.

I urge you, as a parent charged with the protection of your children, to learn how to identify the signs of sexual abuse and how to effectively deal with your child's trauma if he or she becomes a victim. And even more important, take steps to learn how to prevent your child from becoming a victim. (For ideas, see chapter 5.)

Emotional Abuse

Although emotional abuse is the most prevalent type of child abuse, it is much harder to define and to prove than physical or sexual abuse. Think back over your lifetime; I can almost guarantee that you'll remember times of emotional abuse.

Did your parents discipline you in a way that made you feel shamed and guilty? Has anyone ever called you "stupid," "stumble-bum," "mean," "fat," "skinny," "a failure," or some other derogatory name? Did someone laugh at you mockingly? Were you ever a scapegoat?

All these are forms of emotional abuse. The extent of damage done by emotional abuse depends on its source and duration. It's one thing when a complete stranger calls you clumsy and stupid; it's another when your mother does.

Every Saturday for years I dusted the nine rooms in our farm home. I really didn't mind the job, though I'd rather have read a book. Yet somehow I could never get it done right. I remember waking up in the morning, vowing that this would be the day I would finally succeed; Mom would at last be proud of my dusting.

The trouble was, that never happened. Instead, I would be scolded or belittled. "Why, Gracie," Mom would say, "you couldn't have touched this table with the dust cloth!" Somehow she'd always find a few flecks of dust. There would follow longer or shorter tirades about my being a careless, lazy, and irresponsible person. She missed the truth that I was a pretty good kid; I simply couldn't meet her standards.

My mother abused me emotionally. She degraded my person instead of helping me do a better job. If my godly mother could abuse me so, I'm certain many other parents also emotionally and verbally abuse their families. If you recognize yourself as one of them, make a commitment to stop now!

After I spoke on motivation to a high school PTA group, a worried-looking couple approached me and asked, "What can we ever do to motivate our sixteen-year-old son? He's capable enough, but he just won't study. His room's a mess, and his attitude—well, it's unbearable!"

I had just spent an hour discussing how to motivate kids, so I had to pray for patience! Then I asked, "What have you already tried?"

Almost tearfully, the father responded, "Well, I try to make him study. I point out his mistakes. I remind him that he'll never make it, he'll be nothing but a ditchdigger. I can't see how he'll ever make a living."

I'd heard enough. Teenagers intensely want their parents to be proud of them, but their fierce determination to be independent keeps them from ever admitting it to their parents. In his desire to motivate his son, this incredibly concerned but uninformed father had been emotionally abusing him—and unintentionally fueling his rebellion.

Labels and negative predictions may now and then motivate a child to prove a parent or adult wrong, but far more commonly they become self-fulfilling prophecies. I once heard Dr. Haim Ginott, a well-known child psychologist in the 1970s, give an illustration of this concept in a seminar I attended:

A father took his five-year-old son to the ice cream store. When the server handed the ice-cream cone to the dad, the little boy, who wasn't good at waiting, pleaded for it. The father shook his head. "If I give it to you now, you'll just drop it," he said. "No, I won't," the boy promised. "Please give it to me, Daddy!" The father gave his son several more warnings before he finally handed him the ice-cream cone—which the boy immediately dropped.

Dr. Ginott concluded his story with these words: "This child did not want to be an S.O.L. (son of a liar), so he did what Dad repeatedly had said he would do; he dropped the ice-cream cone."

After writing my book *Verbal Abuse*, I received a troubling letter from a physician. His son, an excellent, hardworking swimmer, was on a swim team. The father wrote that the swim coach had never praised the team, no matter how hard the kids tried. This coach wanted a super team, and he seemed to believe that put-downs, yelling, and labeling would motivate his swimmers and make him a champion coach. In reality, the physician's son was discouraged, and his performance had actually declined rather than improved.

Emotional abuse can range from a silent, scathing look to a verbally vile tirade. Its results include lack of confidence, fear, poor achievement, failures, loss of self-esteem, social anxieties—the list goes on.

I have observed that there are two particularly insidious types of emotional abuse, and I would be remiss if I did not address them here: *neglect* and *emotional incest*.

Neglect. Here are some scenarios that portray the numerous ways parents can neglect a child:

- Two-year-old Laura hits Kyle, her four-year-old brother, when she wants his toy. When her mother picks her up to get her ready for dinner, Laura kicks her, too, screaming, "No dinner! I wanna play." Both times Mom excuses her because "she didn't have a very long nap." Mom doesn't like to levy consequences. It's easier to make excuses.

- Three-year-old Annie loves to color and create things from bright paper. She learned some of these crafts in preschool. Dad's at work for long days and Mom has a big house to keep up, a part-time job, and countless duties to accomplish. Both find it's much easier to park Annie in front of the TV than to spend the time and energy to help her be creative.
- Six-year-old Carl needs a little extra help to master his numbers and the alphabet. His single mom has to work a lot and gets no help from anyone. She feels she must keep up her household chores because her mother is so critical when things aren't just so. She'd like to help Carl with his schoolwork, but decides he'll just have to learn from his teacher. Of course, no one teaches Carl to play soccer or softball, because Dad rarely bothers even to see him.
- Bill, grade five, plays sports fairly well. He needs his dad to practice with him so he can really feel confident, but Dad travels for work and when he's home he's really tired. He likes to watch sports on ESPN, but, no, he doesn't feel like pitching a few balls. And he really can't be expected to spend two hours Saturday afternoon in the hot sun watching Bill strike out at his game ...

As horrible and heartbreaking as any kind of abuse is, my heart breaks most for the children of neglect. How hurtful not to be sought out by your parents, or to be avoided or considered too much trouble. Dear Parent, do not *ever* neglect your child. It dehumanizes, traumatizes, and creates despair.

I've worked with several dads who suffered neglect when

they were young. One tried to learn mechanical skills from his father when he was an early teen. A bit awkward, he would drop a wrench or lose a bolt, which frustrated his dad. "Let me do it, Son," his dad would tell him. "You're just no good at a man's job." Not only was this father verbally abusive, he also neglected one of his most important tasks: to patiently teach his son a man's role.

Another dad I know has major difficulty sticking with a job. He evades responsibility whenever possible, does the least he can, and lives for the evenings and weekends when he can play. Though he does play with his sons, the family suffers from his inability to keep a job. When I asked him about his boyhood, he told me that after school he was always anxious to play with his friends. He'd drop off his books and rush out the door, yelling, "I'm going out to play, Mom!" His mom wanted him to be responsible, so she'd yell back, "Not before you clean your room, Michael!"

But Mike was already long gone. And guess what! When he returned, sunburned and mosquito bitten, Mom had cleaned his room for him. She was irritated and he felt horribly guilty—but he'd had fun. Her neglect in proper discipline created an irresponsible, fun-loving, and guilt-ridden man.

Neglecting a child's care, love, and training is abuse, and it exacts a high cost. On the other hand, recognizing that your child is feeling neglected and responding to his or her feelings appropriately is an act of love that can tender great rewards.

Melanie's mother, for instance, found that after baby Neil was born, when Melanie was only eighteen months old, her older child became aggressive and very hard to live with. Melanie didn't want a brother and had no idea what to do with him. At times she would pinch the baby. At other times, while her mother was nursing Neil, she would pull out all the pots and pans from the kitchen cupboards or make a mess of the cosmetics in the bedroom.

Fortunately, her mom understood that Melanie's own needs for babying had not been sufficiently met before her brother had arrived. She asked her mother for help with the baby and returned to her earlier habits of mothering Melanie. She rocked and sang to her, tickled and cuddled her. In only a few weeks, Melanie became resaturated with love and began to have fun watching her rapidly growing brother. Only a few years later, the two children have become dear friends.

Emotional Incest. Ben's father, Al, traveled extensively as a vice president in a large corporation. He loved his family, but showed his love primarily by providing a luxurious lifestyle for them. Almost every Sunday evening he'd tell Ben, "This week I'm staying at the Americana Hotel in New York City. If you need anything, be sure to call me there."

When Ben told me this, I could sense his derision: "Call my dad in New York City to talk about my girlfriend, Cindy? Not on your life! He doesn't care, anyway."

At the time, I was the director of a home for unmarried mothers. Ben's girlfriend, Cindy, lived there because she was expecting their child. At ages fourteen and fifteen they were not capable of raising a child, and with a brave and wise sort of maturity, they planned to give their baby up for adoption.

In the course of our conversations, I learned that this was not the first child Ben had fathered. I began to get a clear picture of the family dynamics. Ben's mother, Callie, had about as much intimacy and time with Al as their children did.

Her husband left most of the household responsibilities and decisions up to her. As Ben grew, his mom found herself becoming increasingly dependent on him. She welcomed his assistance and respected his advice.

In time, Ben replaced her husband's role in Callie's life. She had no emotional boundaries with her son, and showed him lots of affection and attention. Although Callie would never have dreamed of having sex with her son, on a subconscious level she had given Ben her husband's place in her heart.

The closeness of their relationship aroused Ben sexually, and he began to have sexual fantasies about his mother. Ben never attempted to act out his desires with his mother, but he did turn to his girlfriends to act them out. Soon he began to manipulate his girlfriends into having sex with him regularly.

If Ben and Callie had engaged in sexual intercourse, it would be called "incest," and I would have had to report it to the state by law. Even though there is no law against emotional incest, it is clearly very damaging and affects a person's ability to have intimate and caring relationships as an adult.

Emotional incest can also occur between daughters and dads. While working at the home for unwed mothers, I met many young women who engaged in sex in order to act out the fantasies they were having about their fathers. When a dad falls in love with a daughter, he unwittingly indulges her, compliments her, and worst of all, takes sides with her against her mother. The daughter wins, and Mom is hurt and angry and becomes a jealous rival for Dad's attention.

Mom and Dad, keep your commitment to each other foremost. Never let a child displace one of you in the other's heart. Stick together, and you will put one more piece of armor in place to protect your child from abuse.

Spiritual Abuse

I approach this topic with great caution and a plea to my readers for an open mind. Today we live in a culture of permissiveness—an "anything goes" philosophy, even within the church. We stand in jeopardy of losing touch with the Holy One of Israel whose commandments establish the core of all Law. It is crucial that we fix the two ends of this seesaw squarely on the fulcrum of mercy that balances the extremes of law versus license.

A dear friend, Irene, recently opened my eyes to the existence of religious abuse. At forty she told me she had been sexually abused by her youth minister in her early teens. Yet she went on to say that the sexual abuse was not as damaging as something that occurred between her and a Sunday school teacher:

Her teacher had emphasized that no one could ever go to heaven without having accepted Jesus Christ. My friend is a thoughtful and caring person, and at age fourteen could not understand how a loving God could send someone to hell because he had never heard of Jesus Christ. Instead of allowing my friend to ask questions and to pray for the Holy Spirit to work in her life, the teacher became irate and implied that Irene was en route to hell for disagreeing with her.

This example demonstrates how different kinds of abuse can be intertwined, compounding the pain. The Sunday school teacher challenged Irene's intelligence as well as her faith. She was so rigid that Irene felt helpless and stupid and certainly confused. Emotional abuse also had a place in this complex mix, making healing difficult even twenty-five years later.

Becoming a Champion of Children

Although therapy can help bring about healing for victims of child abuse, in general, abuse destroys the potential for a positive and productive life. Far better to prevent the abuse in the first place than to have to deal with its consequences.

We must find ways to prevent the abuse of our children. Jesus Christ said, "But if anyone leads astray one of these little children who believe in me he would be better off thrown into the depths of the sea with a millstone hung around his neck" (Mt 18:6, PHILLIPS).

In the succeeding chapters, you will find down-to-earth methods to prevent all types of child abuse. You will also find some common-sense steps to forgiveness and healing for both abusers and the victims of abuse. My purpose and hope is that every reader will become a champion of children.

2

Is Your Child Safe With YOU?

A woman of great faith who taught Bible studies and Sunday school classes, Corie was pretty, well-dressed, well-loved, and well-respected. I never would have guessed her secret, had she not confessed it to me decades later.

Her son, the younger of her two children, had been especially difficult to raise. Strong-willed and energetic, he could create more messes in ten minutes than she could clean up in hours. To make matters worse, he reminded her of her older brother, Adam, who had tormented her all of their growing up years. Adam had performed the meanest acts and somehow had always convinced their parents that she was the culprit.

At some point, Corie's frustration with her child got the better of her. Frustrated beyond reason with his behavior, she began spanking him. It wasn't discipline; she confessed to me that spanking her son made her feel as if she were finally getting even with her brother. The spankings became more severe.

Corie was finally shocked into confronting her abusive treatment of her son by the horrible bruises on his little legs. Fortunately, she got help to stop the physical abuse, but even years later, tears filled her faded brown eyes and spilled down her wrinkled cheeks as she told me she'd give anything if she could undo those severe spankings.

Then there was Art, well educated, with a highly successful business. From the outside, his family looked happy and healthy. But Art had a deep, dark secret. Try as he might, he couldn't escape the secret, nor could any amount of business success help him shed his profound sense of inadequacy. He enjoyed spending time with his daughters more than he did with his peers because he didn't feel inferior around them. They looked up to him and respected him.

When one of his daughters was twelve, Art started "tucking her into bed" at night. Though his behavior made her uneasy, she pretended to like Dad's special attention. After all, he let her do anything she wanted and gave her everything she asked for. She never had to do chores, even though her sisters did. She tolerated his sexual abuse because of the special treatment it gained her.

Eventually, of course, the situation exploded. The incest came to light and child welfare stepped in. They removed Art from his home and asked me to meet with him.

Art didn't suddenly decide to have sex with his daughter. Like other parents who sexually abuse their children, Art had been abused by his father as a boy. His father had bullied and beaten him, and his sympathetic mother had tried to rescue and protect him. As a result, he never felt like a man. When he married, Art chose a strong woman who also bullied him. He felt so powerless that he viewed his three adolescent daughters as his equals. Art loved his daughter and had not intended to hurt her. Nevertheless, he did. Ignorance is no excuse.

Eric's story is another sad one. I met him as a nine-year-old while I was working as a psychiatric consultant in the public schools. He was the oldest of three boys, all of whom came to school every day dirty, hollow-eyed, and hungry. The staff loved them, cleaned them up, and even provided proper clothing, but the next day they were as disheveled as ever.

One Friday, Eric confided in the caring school counselor. With tears in his eyes he told her that his mother had only a quarter, and they had no food in the house. "What can we do until Monday when we can get lunch at school?" he asked.

When the counselor explored the situation, she discovered that both parents drank heavily and smoked pot. Dad was gone most of the time, and Mom spent most of her time in bed.

Fortunately, the school was able to contact the boys' grandparents, who agreed to take the neglected children over the weekend. Later, a welfare agency intervened.

Abusive parents often love the children they hurt and don't intend to harm them—yet they do. The parents in these examples inflicted terrible damage on their children. Even with increased awareness, abuse still occurs far too widely—even in Christian homes.

The Parent's Role Is Key

Child abuse in America continues to increase. Reports of abuse and neglect rose 9 percent from 1993 to 1997; confirmed reports rose 3 percent in those same four years. In 1997, approximately three children died every day in the United States from abuse or neglect, up 34 percent from 1985. In 1998, more than one million cases of child abuse and neglect were confirmed. Of those, 54 percent were cases of severe neglect; physical abuse accounted for 19 percent; 10 percent of victims suffered sexual abuse and 3 percent severe emotional abuse. (Emotional abuse is difficult to define and in many cases impossible to prove, or that figure would be even larger.) The remaining 14 percent of cases comprised other "miscellaneous" abuses.[1]

When a parent abuses a child, the child suffers multiple injuries. But perhaps his or her most profound injury is the loss of a nurturing, protective parent. Loving parents do not violate their children; they protect them. They do not destroy irreplaceable innocence; they do everything they can to preserve their child's dignity and safety. They don't exploit their own child for selfish gratification.[2]

Your child's safekeeping and nurture is one of your primary tasks as a parent. If your child is not safe with you, he or she will be vulnerable to all sorts of abuse from the rest of the world. You are the most important key in making your child abuse-proof, and it's critical that you be absolutely honest with yourself about your potential to abuse your child.

Do You Have the Potential to Be an Abusive Parent?

Following is a list of questions to help you identify whether you have the potential to abuse a child. Try to keep from feeling defensive and answer these questions honestly.

1. *Do you suffer excessive stress from a variety of sources, from which you are unable to find relief?* If so, ask for support from family, friends, or neighbors. If no one is willing or able to help you out, go to a local child welfare or mental health agency (listed in the Yellow Pages of your phone book) and ask for help there. If you can afford it, go to a family therapist. Help is not easy to find, but it is out there. You must take the responsibility to ask for it.

2. *Were you abused as a child?* Your parents may have meant well, but if they abused or neglected you, you are likely to

repeat their mistakes. You may even have convinced yourself that you deserved their abuse or that overcoming it made you the success you are. Don't believe those deceptions. No child deserves or asks to be beaten, burned, sexually molested, emotionally scarred, or severely neglected.

How a child was abused does not necessarily determine the type of abuse he may perpetrate, but one thing is clear: abuse breeds abuse.

According to a study I vividly recall but cannot locate, abused children will take one of two paths as adults: they will either identify with and follow in the footsteps of their abuser, or they will act in complete opposition to their abuser. Either extreme can create problems. Let me explain.

When I was small, my mother screamed at us dreadfully. I now understand that she did so because she intensely—and mistakenly—wanted us to be perfect so that we would go to heaven. I have forgiven her, but I still remember how I felt then. After one of her unbearable lectures, I would go to my bed, bury my face in a soft comforter, and silently weep out my shame and helplessness. When my emotions had subsided, I would think, "If I ever have a child, I will never yell at her!"

That became a commitment that I usually followed with our three kids. But when my oldest daughter became a teen, she said to me one day, "Mom, I think you oughta yell at us a little more!" And she was right. In my desire not to hurt my children emotionally, I had become too lenient with them.

It seems, at times, that the victim of child abuse can't win—but with patience, effort, and an open mind, you can find that priceless, workable balance between the extremes of total identification with and total opposition to the actions of your abuser.

If you were emotionally, sexually, or physically abused as a child, you may need help to work through your pain and to learn how to treat your child in healthy and nurturing ways. Talk to your pastor or a professional counselor about getting help.

With God's help, you can change; you can relearn perceptions and behavior. Take heart. You are not doomed to repeat the sins of your parents.

3. Do you suffer from low self-esteem? Do you often feel an intolerable sense of helplessness? If so, you could unwittingly be trying to compensate by becoming excessively angry and acting out your feelings through abuse.

Most child abusers do not feel good about themselves. They believe they are incompetent, even helpless. When they are angry and yelling at or hitting a child, they temporarily feel powerful. The child is completely at their mercy, and for as long as the abuse goes on, the abusers continue to feel powerful; for once, they are in control. When the abuse is over, however, they are filled with guilt and remorse. They may vow they'll never do it again. They may even apologize. Yet the next time they feel powerless, they abuse again.

If this description fits you, you may need professional help. Don't delay in finding it. In addition, as you read chapter 3 on building self-esteem, think about the concepts in regard to yourself. Practice focusing on all of your good points. Remember you are a child of God, created in his image. You needn't become arrogant, but learn to accept that in the eyes of God, your worth is great.

4. Do you struggle with social and financial problems? Many studies indicate that child abuse is far more prevalent among lower socioeconomic levels.[3] Child abuse occurs in low-income families (below $15,000 per year) at three times the rate it occurs in moderate-income families ($15,000 to $30,000 per year), and at twenty-five times the rate it occurs in families in the upper-income brackets. These figures have held steady for some twenty years.

Poverty-stricken families face extreme stressors, including unemployment or highly unrewarding jobs, below-standard housing, and unsafe neighborhoods that mirror back to the parents their own sense of ugliness and helplessness. People in such circumstances—both parents and children—have little hope for anything better, and often have no motivation or energy to try to make changes. As noted earlier, abusing their kids can give vulnerable moms and dads a transient sense of power: when the children cower and comply, the parents gain, for at least a short time, a feeling of control.

If you feel economically trapped and see no way out of your situation, understand that how you're feeling is not the objective truth of your circumstances. Help is available. Again, ask family, friends, or neighbors for support. If none of them can or will help, go to a local child welfare or mental health agency (listed in the Yellow Pages of your phone book) and ask for help there. State employment, child welfare, and vocational rehabilitation agencies have excellent programs that can help you get training for and placement in a good job.

5. If you were abused, do you see too much of your abuser in one or more of your children? If one of your children reminds you of an abusive person in your life, you are at high risk to take out on your child all the frustrations your abuser aroused in you. Your child is helpless, as you once were, and without thinking, you can feel it's safe to let your anger be displaced on him or her.

If this is the case for you, first you must fully forgive your abuser. Seek the help of a pastor or counselor if you can't do it alone. You need the accountability and support. You will see your child in a more loving light once the forgiveness is complete.

6. Do you abuse alcohol or other drugs? I have worked with chemically dependent people; I know how good their chemical crutches make them feel and how horrible they feel without their drugs. Their addiction takes priority over everything: their desire to be a good parent, their common sense, their responsibilities. They sink lower and lower into self-pity, weakness, and a childish sort of self-focus.

In 1999, 3.9 million children in the U.S. were living with their grandparents. That's up 75 percent since 1970. Many of the biological parents are chemically dependent and can't or won't give up their habits.[4]

Thank God for the millions of grandparents who fill in for their addicted children. Just at the time they should be retiring and enjoying great freedom, these men and women once again assume the responsibilities of parenting. The challenge can be difficult; often their grandchildren are scarred by the abuse and neglect they've already suffered.

If you abuse drugs and alcohol, you are also abusing your kids. Yet you can change. It takes heroic willpower, lots of help, and enormous tenacity, but it can be done. I strongly recommend Alcoholics Anonymous and Narcotics Anonymous, programs that have the highest success rate known for redeeming addicts. Or perhaps you need to enter an intensive treatment program. Let your needy child, who yearns for your love, be your motivator. Your heavenly Father will help if you'll ask and follow his guidance.

7. Do you focus on yourself instead of others? Are you emotionally immature? Are you able to express your feelings in a controlled manner? Can you postpone your immediate selfish pleasure for the future good of everyone around you? Do you adapt easily to change? Are you able to both give and receive love?

If you answered no to most of these questions, you may need professional help in order to grow up emotionally. In the meantime, try to respond thoughtfully to others—especially to your kids—instead of reacting impulsively in anger or frustration. Express your feelings helpfully instead of destructively. Take care of yourself so you can take care of your children.

8. Do you know when you're getting angry? Do you know how to control your anger? People who know how to express their anger in healthy ways don't hurt others when they feel angry. The next time you get mad at one of your kids, instead of "taking it out" on him or her, try the following:

- Name how you feel. "I'm irritated!" (A little bit angry.) "I'm really mad!" (More angry.) "I'm absolutely furious!" (Greatly angry.) Naming your feelings puts your mind in charge of them.
- Define clearly why you are angry. "I've told you many times to put your dirty clothes in the hamper. And now you expect me to wash your jeans at bedtime! I'm furious!" Often a current problem is similar to one from your past. At the time you first experienced it, you were probably helpless. Now you're not.
- Decide what positive thing you will do about the event that triggered your rage: "I will not stay up late to wash your jeans. You may wear them soiled or wash them yourself." Notice you can still give your child a choice.

If this process seems strange or "stupid" to you, you may have an anger problem. Seek professional help or find an anger management class. It's easy to tell others where they can take their problem and what they can do with it; it takes great maturity to gain control of your feelings first. Before you deal with an issue involving your child, get your anger under control.

9. Are your expectations of your child unrealistic and unfair? Many parents want unrealistic success for their kids. Often this desire is more for the parent's ego than for the child's good. On the other hand, the push for success may be motivated by altruism: some parents may simply want their children to have easier lives than they did.

Whatever the reason behind them, step back and take a good look at your expectations for your children. Ask a teacher what your children's academic and athletic abilities are, and don't demand that they achieve more than they realistically can. And remember, compliment your children for their accomplishments, however small, to help them develop a sense of self-esteem.

10. Are your family relationships uncomfortable? Don't forget that if your child resembles a relative or a spouse who has hurt you in the past, it's easy to take out on him or her the resentment you inevitably feel toward your abuser. If you forgive and let go of that old hurt and resentment, you will be free to love your child—and even the one who abused you.[5]

11. Do you live in a miserable marriage? Just as hurts from members of the family in which you grew up spill out and hurt your child, so can wounds from an abusive spouse. If a child seems too much like a difficult spouse, you may unknowingly hurt that child.

12. When your child misbehaves, do you find yourself feeling inadequate, even helpless? And do you unwittingly resort to rage to compensate for your helplessness? There are better ways to correct your children than venting your rage on them. See chapter 4 on discipline for specific ideas.

13. Do you put your feelings and needs ahead of your child's? All behaviors have meanings and are connected with needs. You will fail to meet your children's deep needs if you focus only on your need for power. If, for example, you need your child to respond to your requests instantly, you are very likely missing something—specifically, the unmet needs at the root of his or her misbehavior. Look beyond yourself to discover why your child misbehaved and work on that root cause; you will be far more effective in correcting the behaviors.

14. Are you secure in your sexual identity? When parents have issues of confusion about their own sexual identity, they may use their children to attempt to clarify their sexuality. A mother, for example, who grew up being punished for curiosity about genitalia may examine her children's sexual organs and may even touch them needlessly and excessively because she is still curious. The same dynamic, of course, holds true for a father treated similarly as a boy.

If you need help in this area, don't victimize your children by using them to teach yourself about sexuality. Seek out a professional counselor who can help you work out these important issues. You need to understand your body and how it functions sexually and physiologically.

Satisfy your curiosity by reading, attending a class, or talking with your doctor or nurse. If you have uncomfortable sexual feelings or urges, use all the willpower you have to control them. If you even think that you want to touch a child in a sexual way, run as fast as you can in the opposite direction and get help.

You need a well-trained person who can help you eradicate the unhealthy urges you may feel. The process will take time. It will cost money, and it will be mighty uncomfortable. No matter. Do it to the finish. It may well keep you out of prison. For sure, it will save any possible victim, as well as yourself, a lifetime of sorrow and remorse.

15. Do you feel isolated and alone? Any parent who has to struggle alone with life's responsibilities suffers great stress. In my personal experience, it is a kind of stress likely to result in child neglect.

I've known Virginia for decades. She is intelligent but uneducated. She and her unemployed husband had seven children before he abandoned all of them. My friend worked hard to pay rent on a run-down house and keep her children fed and clothed, even minimally. But she could not marshal her resources to do more, even to show affection or to discipline or train them.

Virginia told me: "When I get home from work, I sit in my easy chair and read. My seven kids gather around me, yelling and fighting with each other; they even hit me sometimes. But I just tune 'em out. I can't do any more." While I understood her desperate state, I predicted the outcome accurately. Five of her seven lovely but severely neglected children became wards of the state. One served time in prison.

If you're facing life alone, you need to find a support group that can bolster your spirits and hold you accountable as a parent. You can seek support from public agencies such as state child welfare. In most cities there is a Salvation Army community service resource or a gospel mission that offers rich resources to families like Virginia's.

Tragically, many Virginias haven't the hope or the energy to reach out for help to these agencies and organizations. We need volunteers to organize outreach efforts to these struggling souls. If one person had visited Virginia even once a week, helped her clean house, taken care of her kids for a while—what a difference it could have made!

If You Need Help

If you realize after reading the preceding section that you have stepped over the line into abuse—or that you have the potential to—I recommend that you take the following steps:

1. *Admit to yourself and to your spouse that you have abused your children or that you fear you might.* I have often sat with weeping parents as even late in life they have finally reached this deep honesty. It hurt. But only then could they even begin to seek forgiveness and be reconciled with their children.

2. *Identify the reason behind your abusive behavior.* When you can find healing for your own old hurts, you'll be less likely to hurt anyone else. And when you can acknowledge your erroneous perceptions, you can correct them. Right thinking produces right methods and actions.

3. *When you are under excessive stress, verbalize that fact to your family.* In the years I worked as a pediatrician, I knew immeasurable stress on many days. Routinely on such days I would say something like this to my three children: "Kids, I've had a dreadful day and I'm really tired. I need you to help me by being really good. If I have to correct you, I'm probably going to be very grouchy!" Not perfectly, but in great measure, it worked. They loved me, but they also wanted to protect themselves from my grouchiness!

4. *Make peace with yourself and with your abusers.* Try to understand why and how they became abusive. Let go of your old hurts, forgive the people who hurt you, and move on. For detailed ideas on forgiving, consult a resource such as my book, *When You Can't Say "I Forgive You"* (Colorado Springs: Nav Press, 2000).

5. *If trying to understand your abusive behavior is too much for you on your own, seek outside counsel.* Look for a therapist who understands family dynamics. Work with him or her until you are free from the old tapes that have been so destructive for you. Such freedom will help prevent you from passing on your hurts to your children—you can count on it.

Many good people abuse their kids out of ignorance, or as a result of defective parenting across generations, or because of a breakdown during overwhelming stress. Every parent needs to take an inventory regularly to determine if they have unwittingly crossed the line into abuse.

"Who, me?" you ask. "Yes, you!" I reply. You'll be so relieved to learn you have not abused your child. And I trust you'll be even more comforted if your inventory stops abusive behavior that you may never even have realized was harming your child.

3

Building Your Child's Self-Esteem

Shelley lived consistently in the sunshine. She was no beauty queen, but her dark blonde hair was always shiny clean and her gray eyes twinkled with an inner joy. She worked hard to get good grades and to be a good team member. Best of all, she was kind to her classmates and was a friend to be trusted—none of the "I'm your best friend today but don't count on me tomorrow."

Shelley's dad invested his love, wisdom, and strength in her life. He was convinced she could achieve anything she wanted, and he communicated his confidence to her.

Shelley's mom taught her how to do the household chores, and she learned that she was competent. Though Mom was a strict disciplinarian who on occasion lectured her daughter, she also loved her dearly. If Shelley was hurt because a jealous classmate ignored her, Mom comforted her.

Mom and Dad both disciplined their daughter's childhood mistakes, but they made it clear she had great worth in spite of her faults. When Shelley achieved only a red ribbon at the spring track meet, her family cheered as intensely as if it were blue. Later, her dad helped her practice and gave her pointers to improve her strategy.

Shelley knew her parents loved her no matter what. If her parents were too busy to supply her needs for affection or attention, she felt secure enough to let them know what she needed: "Mom, I need a hug and time to talk." Or, "Dad, I missed you at my track meet. I need you to cheer for me!"

Of course Shelley had her share of bumps and bruises in life, but her solid foundation of healthy self-respect held her steady through the rough times. With her protective and nurturing home life and strong self-esteem, Shelley was unlikely to become a victim of abuse.

Marvin's story is just the opposite. His permissive parents allowed him to play in the nearby woods any time he chose. Mom nagged him now and then about doing his chores, but if he didn't do them, she irritably did them for him. Marvin felt her constant disapproval, but he loved to play; acceptance of her anger seemed a small price to pay. He rationalized that Mom was "always grumpy anyway." At least he had freedom in his tree house in the woods.

Since Marvin stayed out of trouble as a young boy, his parents weren't forced to be involved in his life. No one paid much attention to him, or even noticed him most of the time. His father, a salesman, traveled two or three days a week, and when he was home, he spent little time with his son; he had reports to file, or he was too tired, or he was trying to make Mom happy. He rarely came to his son's soccer games, and had no idea that Marvin was not doing well at school.

Marvin had no idea how to stand up for himself, and he desperately craved acceptance. By age ten, he felt weak and scared, and began hanging out with members of a local gang. He found their swagger strong and protective, and it seemed better to join them than to be victimized by them.

Marvin was instead a victim of his parents—a victim of abusive neglect. In effect, his parents abandoned him. No wonder he gravitated toward bullies and gangs! He needed something or someone to help him feel important. He is still, at eighteen, making only a borderline adjustment in life—and his parents seem oblivious to his struggles.

Parents have great influence over their child's self-esteem—for good or bad. As a parent, you can nurture the development of specific qualities that will strengthen your children's self-respect and self-esteem, which will, in turn, help to abuse-proof them.

Parents can help build their children's sense of their own worth in a number of ways: by extending unconditional acceptance, by acting in predictable ways, by balancing approval and disapproval, by offering grace instead of guilt, and by helping their children experience success.

Offer Unconditional Acceptance

My father loved us all dearly, but he rarely touched us or gave us hugs. Instead, he gave us love through his eyes. Decades after his death, I can still recall the twinkle of his brown eyes when some surprise or mischief was coming. I can still see the somber worry when there was not enough money during the Great Depression, the anxiety when my brother was drafted into the navy in World War II, the spark of anger when one of us misbehaved or some injustice had occurred in our community. God said, "I will guide thee with mine eye" (Ps 32:8). Because my dad did just that, I know what that verse means. And I know that both my father and my heavenly Father love me unconditionally.

To communicate unconditional acceptance:

- Love your child tenaciously, even at his or her worst.
- Set limits and enforce them. When your child misbehaves, follow through consistently with appropriate consequences—

but distinguish between the child and the child's behavior, and communicate that distinction to your child.

- Seek to understand the reasons for misbehavior—rather than simply assume your child is stubborn or disobedient. (More on this in chapter 4 on discipline.)
- Correct your child's mistakes and misbehavior lovingly. Children learn and grow from corrective instruction, which bolsters their self-confidence and polishes skills that help them feel competent.
- Forgive your child's misbehavior promptly. *Do understand that forgiving is not excusing bad behavior.*
- Praise the job well done.
- Tell your child "I love you." Often. I don't think those words can ever be said too many times.
- Talk to your child. Give positive feedback and communicate positive ideas.
- Read to your children. Sing with them. Choose positive, upbeat books and songs.
- Show your child affection. A psychologist friend of mine says that children need over two hundred loving touches daily. I don't know where he came up with that figure, but I like the idea. Children need to have their heads touched, their backs patted (and sometimes scratched or gently rubbed), their ears playfully tweaked, their feet tickled, and their bodies hugged—playfully and with love.
- BUT—if you have sexual thoughts or feelings about a child, *do not touch that child.* Trust me, children will sense it if you have sexual feelings toward them. If this is the case for you, get help. A competent counselor who knows the concepts of family therapy can teach

you to be a healthy parent able to provide your children with the appropriate affection they need.

In all your interactions with them, show your kids unconditional acceptance in both your words and deeds. In as many ways as you can, tell your kids, "Hey, I love you. You are of infinite worth."

Be Predictable

When our three children were all in school, mornings were hectic. I had to get three pairs of matching shoes together while fixing breakfast and watching for the school bus. Some mornings went well and everyone got off to school happy. Other mornings, however, I found myself scolding, hurrying, and even yelling at my children. On those days I went to work feeling miserable because I had vowed I would never yell at my kids. I'm sure they felt both sad and mad, and had less than the good day I wished for them.

It finally occurred to me that my inconsistency was behind all those bad starts, so I began to discipline myself. I'm not a morning person, but I made myself get up a little earlier than usual, and went to each child's bed to kiss or gently tease them awake. I put a bit of a candied cherry or an M & M on their toast or cereal and sat with them as we focused on a bit of Scripture and a short prayer before they ran out the door.

Once my kids learned that I would be the same nurturing mom every day (well, nearly every day!), they became settled instead of anxious and could even give back the love I showered on them. How much better our days and lives were, and how much more self-worth my children had because I showed them their value to me.

Instead of verbally and emotionally abusing my children (and that is what it was, much as I hate to admit it), I learned to abuse-proof them by being predictable in my behavior toward them.

Predictability means that in a given situation that occurs on a regular basis, you react similarly each time. Here are some examples of the ways that parents need to be predictable:

1. When you awaken your child, do so the same way every day. Don't yell from the kitchen one day, and teasingly tousle their hair the next. I recommend going to each one, and gently waking them with loving touches.

2. If your four-year-old keeps asking, "Why do grasshoppers jump?" (or similar unanswerable queries), answer the same way every time. Don't ever discourage questions, though you may need to postpone answering the more difficult ones.

3. When you must correct your child's misbehavior, do so firmly, definitely, and similarly every time: "Don, you may not hit your sister. Sit in time-out, *now,* until you can honestly apologize and figure out how to settle your disagreements without hitting."

Take time to assess how predictable your behavior is with your children. Do you need to make some changes? Don't hesitate to do so.

Balance Approval and Disapproval

Jerry's anxious mother brought him to see me. His preschool teacher was threatening to expel the four-year-old because he was mean to the other children, grabbed toys, called them names, and at times hit or bit them.

As I tried to collect information as to why Jerry behaved so badly, his mom told me that he was simply energetic, and at times was probably tired or not feeling well. She even told me she believed her darling was destined to become a great leader because he was so strong-willed and aggressive. She was convinced that the teachers were biased against her son and that the kids were jealous of his great abilities. Mom, in fact, gave Jerry a sort of worshipful approval that was fast creating a monster.

The fact is, a child won't believe a parent's approval if the parent never shows healthy disapproval. When children are taught boundaries and find that they must live within them, they behave appropriately, which gives them an opportunity to discover the earned approval of others. What a builder of self-esteem that is! Such a child will be far less vulnerable to being abused than children who have no boundaries established for them.

Ronald's parents were the opposite of Jerry's. They expected perfection from their son, and because no one can ever deliver perfection, they never expressed approval of anything Jerry did. His parents constantly scolded him, shamed him, and predicted all kinds of horrors for his future unless he changed. Sometimes Ronald would try to do better, but if he had even one wrong answer on a test at school, his dad would sternly ask him, "Why did you make that stupid mistake?"

Even though he tested as gifted, Ronald was getting Ds and Fs on his school report card. As a last resort, his parents sent Ron to me. As I watched shame, anger, and immense sadness flicker across Ron's young face, I asked him, "Who in your life has ever been proud of you for anything you've done?" Pensively, Ron sat thinking. At last he replied, "I guess my dog is, when I play with him."

No wonder Ronald was failing in school. His parents had

the opposite problem that Jerry's mom had, but were just as unbalanced in their expression of approval and disapproval.

How can you balance approval and disapproval as a parent? Here are some guidelines:

- Have reasonable and fair expectations of your child's scholastic ability. (A teacher can help you know what your child is capable of doing.)
- Teach your child to do age-appropriate chores at home. Work with your child until he or she knows how to do those chores well—and actually does them.
- Set a schedule for chores and make certain your child does them properly. Offer help only when you know it's needed.
- Check on the quality of your child's work. If it's not his or her best, firmly but kindly have the child make corrections. Then, and only then, express your unqualified approval. Point out specific things that are well done and express your genuine appreciation.
- If your child's attitude while doing a chore is terrible, try to ignore it, focusing instead on the quality of the task. Then try your own version of a statement like this: "Janie, I know you hated to clean your room. You'd much rather have been reading. I understand that. But do you know I'm really excited about how neat your room looks? And even more, I'm so proud of you for doing it even when you didn't want to."

Could any child fail to glow inside when a parent picks such good statements out of even a nasty attitude? If you can keep up this habit of praise, you'll find that ugly attitude changing bit by bit.

Take time to think about the ways you express approval and disapproval of your child's behavior. Is your approach balanced?

Give Grace, Not Guilt

Guilt does more damage to self-esteem than anything else. Yet many parents unwittingly correct their children by making them feel exceedingly guilty. Remarks like, "Don't you know how sad you make God feel when you lie to me?" make the child feel like a criminal. How much better it would be to say, "You know, Carey, God would like to help you learn how to be honest. Let's talk about it."

Many years ago, Paul Tournier, a Christian psychiatrist from Europe, wrote a classic book entitled *Guilt and Grace.* The book describes how guilt can motivate change, but that accumulated guilt results in despair and depression. Grace, by contrast, acknowledges the sin but forgives and redeems it. This keeps hope alive.

I have vivid memories of a personal event that makes this principle clear.

In first grade I went to a one-room country school where one teacher somehow managed to teach twenty to twenty-five students in eight grades. The school was very much the focus of our rural community life, and school events drew a packed crowd of parents and neighbors.

That year we worked for weeks on our Christmas program. The night finally arrived, and the program was ready. I was too excited to speak, just full of the joy of this holy season. All the students wore their best Sunday clothes—for most of us in 1932, well-mended hand-me-downs. We had tacked up handmade decorations everywhere. A Christmas tree with real lights stood in a corner; under it were piled small gifts that we had made for each other and for our parents.

The only other student in first grade was a foster child, Patsy, who lived with one of our neighbors. I thought she was beautiful. Her golden hair was all curls, while mine was straight. Her eyes were clear and blue, and her smooth skin resembled that of a store-shelf doll I had seen. I had gray-green eyes and freckles. Her clothes were new and stylish in comparison to my hand-me-downs. Surprisingly, I wasn't jealous of her, but I think I saw her as belonging in a different world.

The night of the Christmas program, Patsy wore a gorgeous outfit, a brown pleated skirt topped with a gold sweater that accentuated her curls. The sweater had a brown collar and a brown yarn bow at the neck that sported two incredibly soft-looking yarn balls. They bounced as she walked, and I couldn't keep my eyes off them.

When it came time for the students to sing carols, Patsy and I, because we were the youngest and smallest, stood in the front row. I missed not a note nor a word, but in the middle of our carols, I couldn't resist reaching over to Patsy and touching those mysterious brown spheres. They were just as soft as they looked. Christmas with all of its mystery and magic had begun.

At breakfast the next morning, I discovered the innocent gesture had horrified my mother, a very proper lady; she gave me a lengthy lecture and told me she was ashamed of me. The totally unexpected scolding left me speechless, sad, and feeling very much alone. All the sparkle and light and excitement of the season were gone. I felt only despair and loneliness.

At last the horrible words stopped and I crept away. Silently

I cowered in a warm corner of our kitchen behind the cookstove. Life was black; Christmas was gone; I was a dreadful person with no hope.

How long I sat in that corner I don't know, but it seemed like an eternity. Finally, I heard footsteps and lifted my eyes to see the well-worn work shoes and faded denim overalls of my father. This amazing man had waited for just the right time. He bent down and scooped me up in his big, strong arms. And then he spoke the words that relit Christmas for me, restoring my hope.

"Gracie," he said softly, "what you did wasn't really so bad. In fact, I thought it was kind of cute!" With a tender kiss and another soft hug, he put me into a whole new world, one in which even the wrong I did could be understood and forgiven. A world of grace. Because of my father, I learned that grace forgives sins and gives us hope that we can overcome them and be a person of value.

While my mother's shaming response crushed me, my father's grace restored my self-esteem and gave me hope that even if I made mistakes, I was loved, valuable, and special. A child who knows that is close to being abuse-proof.

Help Your Child Experience Success

Parents can help even one-year-olds experience the success of accomplishment, another building block of self-esteem.

Millie was not quite a year old when her mother observed her taking all of the toys out of a basket, and then putting them back in the basket. This wise mom capitalized on this typical one-year-old behavior by sitting beside Millie and praising her for picking up all of her toys. She hugged her daughter and helped her clap her hands, applauding her success.

Small wonder that Millie became a neat child who felt proud of herself.

Helping kids achieve success, of course, is not always so easy. Many children have obvious gifts and interests, and for them, success is more likely than not. Others have less apparent interests and are more laid-back and much harder to motivate. Once again, there are ground rules that will help you engineer success for your children:

- Start as early in life as possible. Start now!
- Observe your child in a variety of surroundings and with different objects. See what toys, colors, materials, and activities he or she chooses. Does he love music? Does she enjoy creating new objects from old? What is your child good at? Ask others for input.
- Once you know your child's talents, find games, groups, and guidance that will help her develop them.
- Structure some regular time when your child can grow in his or her special skills; the amount of time, obviously, would depend on age and the ability of the child to focus.
- Avoid pushing too hard or nagging, which spoils the fun and creates resistance.
- If your child has done her best, do not criticize the result. Praise the sincere effort instead.
- Give specific compliments to help your child know the value of his project and his efforts.
- Help your child learn self-control. Do this by avoiding undue attention to your child's negative emotions. Teach her words for sadness, anger, fear, excitement. Help him understand circumstances that prompt such

feelings. Help her figure out how to cope with difficulties and solve problems.

- Help your child learn the discipline of finishing a task. Kids may need breaks during the process, but stick with them until a given job is well done. Then praise them. Teaching your children self-control and self-discipline will develop their skills and build their character.
- Teach your child that failure is an important ingredient of success. Sometimes even the most gifted, hard-working child will fail at a given task. Only people who refuse to push themselves to their limit never fail. Failure can teach us almost as much as success when we evaluate it and learn from it.

So much for building success in areas that a child enjoys and in which she may be gifted. What about the foot-slogging hard work kids uniformly hate to do—cleaning house and doing dishes, yard work, and homework?

- Organize family work days. Working together as a family, perhaps even more than playing together, will bond you, teach mutual respect, and open communication channels. (In the midst of doing some routine tasks my children have opened up and shared their innermost feelings, dreams, and thoughts.) Working together also enables younger kids to learn from older ones and gives parents a chance to teach the best ways to get work done. As always, bragging on both effort and accomplishments will build any child's confidence and awareness of self-worth.

Remember, the closer you are to your kids, even in sharing activities, the safer you and your children will feel with each other—and the more immune to any form of abuse they will be.

4

To Spank or Not to Spank

Some time ago, several juvenile court workers and I spoke to a group of parents and teachers. One of the court workers warned the audience, "If you don't teach your children right from wrong, then we [the courts] will have to ... and we won't be doing it as kindly as you might." Her words were true: the courts deal harshly with juvenile offenders.

Unfortunately, in response to the harsh treatment, many kids rebel even more. How much better for children to learn right from wrong at home, in the hands of firm but loving parents who correct mistakes and misbehavior. Proactive parenting translates into wise, healthy training and discipline—insurance against your child becoming the victim of abuse.

Many people think of discipline as *punishment* meted out to a child in order to correct his or her mistakes or wrongdoings. The truth is, excessively harsh and rigid "discipline" can produce kids who obey others blindly, thus making them susceptible to forceful abusers. These children, fearing their bullying perpetrators, don't even try to resist them. Other children respond to such treatment by rebelling and acting out in ways that end up inviting abusive treatment from others.

But discipline and punishment are not the same thing. In fact, far from punishment, the word *discipline* comes from a Latin term meaning "to teach and to learn."

What does it mean, then, to discipline a child? To answer this question, let's first explore what good discipline is *not.*

What Good Discipline Is Not

Good discipline does not incite fear. One family I knew whipped their preschool-aged child many times a day. They genuinely believed that such punishment would make their gorgeous and spirited child perfect. One day this child's father, who had endured his own share of whippings in his youth, heard his son make a comment that shocked him. His mother had just whipped him for being sassy to her. The child looked up at the mom's angry face. "Well, Mom," he said, "I hope that made you feel better." The wise young dad got the message. Although their intentions were good, their abusive methods were hardening their son's heart.

The apostle Paul wrote, "And, ye fathers, provoke not your children to wrath: but bring them up in the nurture and admonition of the Lord" (Eph 6:4). Sadly enough, parental discipline sometimes becomes terrible child abuse. I exhort you to watch your child's face as you correct him or her. Does she look downright scared? Does he clench his jaws and look angry? If so, you are overshooting the mark.

Good discipline is not blind. Millie has four children and dearly cherishes them. She wants them to be perfect kids but attempts to achieve such perfection by ignoring or excusing their often obnoxious behavior. When Curt is ill-tempered, it's simply because he missed his nap. And when Heather hits her baby brother and grabs his toys, she must be coming down with a cold. (Yes, a bad one!)

Ignoring broken rules and bad behavior makes parenting

easier in the short run. But look ahead, even a little way, and you'll know that such practices only defer the need for correction—and make it infinitely more difficult. Don't shut your eyes and play blind to your child's mistakes.

Good discipline is not tyrannical. Arlene's father made her life difficult. A rigid perfectionist, he was hard on himself and hard on her. He expected everything, from her grades to her style of dress, to measure up to his exacting standards. If she got 95 percent on a spelling test, he would ask, "And what did Wilma get?" If Arlene's hair was not in perfect order, he would comb it for her.

At first Arlene was fearful of her dad, avoiding him whenever she could. But by the time she was twelve, unwilling to put up with her father's tyranny any longer, she began to talk back and rebel in silent, sneaky ways.

Parental dictatorship results in one of two outcomes—either the child will withdraw in sullen fear or rebel in secret and, later, blatant ways. In any case, tyrannical parenting makes children susceptible to abuse from others.

Good discipline doesn't sweat the small stuff. Phil was an only child until he was eleven. An energetic, impulsive boy, he seemed to be in big trouble much of his life. The problem was, his parents nitpicked everything he did. If he scratched his ear the wrong way, they lectured him on how funny it looked. If he wriggled in his chair, they sternly told him, "Phillip, sit still!" If he spilled his milk at dinner, his evening was ruined.

Nitpicking parents, like tyrants, create more rebellion and discouragement than they do compliance and learning. Don't nit-pick! A simple guideline to help you decide if an issue is worth addressing is to ask yourself: Will I remember this issue ten years from now? If I make something big out of it, will my child be a worse or better person for it?

Some issues are important for the long run; others are not. Save your energy for those that will really count in your child's future.

Good discipline is never abusive. When I was only eight, my father taught me a lesson I have never forgotten in all the years since. My job was to carry in wood and kindling each morning for our wood-burning stove. A happy child, I loved to play or read or simply run about with Dad while he did the big chores—and I often conveniently forgot to do the chores I'd been assigned.

It would have been easy for one of my parents to fulfill my responsibilities for me, but they understood how bad that would have been for me. So it was that late one night, my father woke me from a sound sleep and in his no-nonsense voice told me to follow him downstairs. Then, with a stern look but no more words, he took me to the kitchen and pointed to the empty wood box, then to the back door. I got the message.

Shivering in the crisp autumn weather and feeling a bit afraid of the dark, I trudged to the woodpile and lugged in enough fuel for breakfast preparation. Though he did not help me carry the wood, Dad watched from the porch to make sure I didn't stumble.

I learned this lesson from the way my father handled the empty wood box: I must be responsible. I must make wise choices—and playing instead of doing my simple chores was not a wise choice. Lessons like that, executed with both love and a firm hand, give children the strength and ability to reject potentially abusive people and situations.

My father could have spanked and lectured me—but doing so would have wounded my tender, sensitive spirit. I saw two of my brothers rebel against too severe correction. I'm blessed that didn't happen to me.

To Spank or Not to Spank

Twice in my life, my mother spanked me. Both times she walked me through three rooms to a private place, told me clearly what I'd done wrong, and swatted me several times, though not hard.

I hated it, and I was angry with her. But later, once I got over the anger and humiliation, I felt a strange sense of relief, a lightness. Now I know that the relief came because I no longer felt guilty for my disobedience. I'd paid the price, you see, and was no longer the criminal.

Yet, how much better a lesson I would have learned if instead of swatting me, or at least along with it, my mother had made me apologize to my little sister. I wish she had taught me how to make amends, how to treat my sister right.

Being spanked taught me only half a lesson: that what I had done was wrong. My mother missed an opportunity to help me understand why my behavior was wrong, what had motivated it, and how I might have handled myself differently. She also missed the chance to teach me how to right the wrong I'd committed. The truth is that kids often know very well they've misbehaved, but having to verbalize their misbehavior helps them assume personal responsibility for it. It also helps them figure out how to make a change for the better.

A woman of great faith, my mother never meant to be

abusive. But she had a rigid set of standards. She wanted her children to be perfect examples of good Christians, and she applied her demands for that perfection at all levels.

Many people advocate spanking as a biblical mandate for parents, quoting Proverbs 13:24: "He that spareth his rod hateth his son; but he that loveth him chasteneth him betimes." Tragically, some Christian parents have used this verse to justify beating their child. But hitting a child so hard it raises welts or makes bruises is not discipline. Plain and simply, "discipline" that harms a child is abuse.

I strongly disagree with any interpretation of Proverbs 13:24 that gives angry parents permission to practice child abuse under the guise of discipline. Other Bible verses that mention the "rod" shed light on the issue, and speak directly to parents about how they are to teach—that is, to discipline—their children:

"The rod and reproof give wisdom" (Prv 29:15).

"The rod of correction shall drive it [foolishness] far from him" (Prv 22:15).

"Thy rod and thy staff they comfort me" (Ps 23:4).

Does our wise and loving heavenly Father truly prescribe the beating of children by their parents? I don't believe so. In fact, I believe he teaches us in these verses to guide and "prod" our children into good behavior—and to rescue them from dangerous and harmful situations.

First, "the rod" in these verses refers not to an instrument of punishment, but to a shepherd's rod, which was used for very different purposes.

Let me explain with a scene from my childhood. Many hot summer days found me watching my dad's small flock of sheep as they grazed. Our sheep were not supposed to feed in some spots, as the vegetation was toxic to them. I had to keep watch over them and guide them back to safe pastures before they reached the grasses that were bad for them. I always carried a long stick—a rod—to help me do that. I didn't use the rod to beat the sheep; I used it to gently prod them in the right direction. Consistent prodding was all it took to keep them in the right place.

The shepherd's staff used during the time these verses were written was a long pole with a crook on the end. If a sheep fell into a crevice and could not get out, the shepherd grasped one of its legs in the crook of the staff and extricated it. No wonder the rod and staff brought comfort to David, the shepherd-poet who wrote Psalm 23!

Because it is easy for a parent who is frustrated, stressed, or angry to strike a child too hard during a spanking, I strongly recommend that, in general, parents not spank their kids, with a "rod" or with their hand. Instead, I recommend that parents use appropriate consequences when a child misbehaves. Spankings can leave marks on the body, and worse, scars on a child's soul.

Appropriate Consequences

Proactive parenting means setting up logical ground rules for your kids along with fair consequences, related to the "crime," when a ground rule is broken.

For example, Sammy, seven, didn't like to go to bed. Every night after his parents put him down and said his prayers with him, Sammy would invariably get up for a drink, or to use the potty, or to beg for "just one more hug!" His parents realized he was manipulating and even rebelling against their simple rule, "Bedtime is 8:00," so they developed a highly effective consequence: each time Sammy left his bed, he had to go to bed five minutes earlier the following night. They told him the consequence and laid out a pad and pencil where he couldn't avoid seeing it. Each time he got out of bed, they marked it down, and the next night Sammy's bedtime was 7:30. He wailed and objected, but they held firm. Three nights later, Sammy's bedtime was back to 8:00, and he had learned a valuable lesson: Mom and Dad were in charge and he had to respect and obey their rules.

Many parents have difficulty finding appropriate and effective consequences for misbehavior. Here are some of my favorites; you may well have devised your own.

1. Give a time-out. When you give a child a time-out, I recommend that you use this procedure:

Place the child needing correction in a certain chair (the same one every time) within your sight so that she will not feel abandoned. Ask the child to stay there until she can tell you these three things:

What did I do that was wrong?

What should I have done instead?

How will I remember to do the right thing next time?

Preschoolers will need some help answering these questions, but even young children are capable of thinking at this level. When a child answers these questions, he owns the problem, is responsible for it, and figures out a way to solve it on his own.

2. Use physical restraint as needed. At age two, one of my children threw kicking, screaming temper tantrums. If I gave him a time-out, he easily could have hurt himself while flailing around. So instead, I picked him up, kicking and screaming, took him to a big rocking chair, and held him, my legs around his and my arms circling his body and arms. He could wriggle, but he couldn't hurt himself or me.

As I held him, I firmly explained that I loved him too much to let him hurt himself or break his toys. I held him this way until he regained control and let me be the boss. The first time I did this, it took over thirty minutes. But each successive time became shorter, and within three weeks, I rarely had to use this exhausting method. A miracle!

One young mother, after hearing me explain this disciplinary measure at a parents' seminar, told me, "Dr. Grace, my father used that holding technique when I was little. I used to hate it, but I never in my life felt as safe as I did in his strong arms."

3. Requisition toys or revoke privileges. When a child abuses a toy or privilege, I recommend taking away that toy or privilege to teach him how to play with the toy or to respect the privilege.

For example, when preschoolers or elementary school kids fight over a toy or are deliberately destructive with things, you can say, "You know our rule about respecting our toys and each other. You have just broken that rule, so I am taking the toy until you can show me that you can play without fighting or breaking things."

Beware, though, that removing a toy for too long can discourage the child. If he thinks he will never get it back, he won't be motivated to do anything differently. So, as soon as the child takes turns, shares, and shows kindness to his or her playmates, the toy should be returned. But be consistent in enforcing consequences when, or if, the behavior recurs. I recommend keeping a toy from a preschooler for half an hour. For school-aged kids, unless they do not correct their mistakes, keep the toy only a day or two.

Older kids need to have a privilege removed if they abuse it. For example, if your junior high school student comes home after curfew, she should be grounded for several days or lose her phone privileges. Or, if a high schooler gets a speeding ticket, take away his driving privileges for a week or more. And make sure your child—not you—pays the ticket.

4. Give extra work assignments. Kevin, nine, hated to clean his room, so he'd postpone the chore as long as possible. Then, as he finally rushed to "clean" it, griping and complaining, he'd slide stuff under his bed instead of putting it away. His mom's supervision and nagging helped very little.

One day she told him, "Kevin, I can see that your cleaning skills are very poor. You obviously need more practice so we can change that. Instead of cleaning only your room, you'll also be cleaning the garage and the bathroom this week. Dad or I will teach you how to work efficiently. Once you've figured out how it's done, you may go back to cleaning only your own room."

Of course, Kevin fussed and yelled, but his parents held firm. There were none of his usual pleasures on Saturday until the work was done—correctly. Kevin learned obedience, good work skills, responsibility, and self-respect from this routine.

5. Confiscate clothing. Susie's five children, like so many others, often dropped their sweaters in the front entrance, their shoes by the sofa, their schoolbags next to the dining table, and their socks in front of the TV. For some time Susie picked up after them, but one day she decided she'd finally had it.

Instead of returning the abandoned items to her children, Susie filled a huge trash bag with them. In order to redeem their belongings, her children had to buy them back—either with cash or by doing a load of laundry. Over time, they learned that Mom meant business, and they began to take care of their clothes and books.

6. Give kids choices. When your child disobeys you, let him or her choose between obedience or a consequence for disobedience. For example: If your son has a problem coming home late after playing with a friend, tell him, "I'm going to give you a choice. Either come home on time today, or you won't be playing with Jim after school tomorrow." If your daughter has trouble getting her homework done, tell her, "Finish your homework before dinner, or you won't be watching TV after dinner. You'll have to study then."

Remember, the more calmly and matter-of-factly you speak, the better your kids will listen—but only if you follow through!

If Consequences Don't Work

If your child continues to misbehave even after you have tried the methods listed above, as a last resort you may have to administer swats. Here's how to do it without endangering your child's priceless spirit:

- Wait to administer swats until your anger is well under control.
- Explain what the child has done that is wrong and why it's wrong.
- Keep your words few, wise, firm, and loving.
- Administer the swats carefully. When your hand stings, stop!
- Remember, the least severe correction that will effect the needed change is the ideal consequence.
- Give the child private time to consider the entire event and focus on the lesson learned.

- When the episode is over, briefly discuss the lesson, then comfort and hug your child. Children need to know they are forgiven and that there is hope for them.
- Never bring up the past misdeeds of your child. Once forgiven, our sins are removed as far as the east is from the west (see Ps 103:12). So should your child's transgressions be forgotten.

Don't Abuse Your Child in the Name of Discipline

Chapter 2, "Is Your Child Safe With YOU?", addresses some of the reasons that parents end up physically abusing their children and recommends some steps to take for help. If, after reading this chapter, you've realized that you have crossed over the line between discipline and abuse in your efforts to correct your child's mistakes or misbehavior, review chapter 2 and then prayerfully read Proverbs 23:13 *in the light of the shepherd's rod.* Compare the verse to Ephesians 6:4, and ask God to help you find the tough love all parents need when correcting their children—the balance between kindness and firmness that will guide them and teach them without breaking their spirits.

Most of all, get to know yourself. When you are exhausted and worried and tension is running high, take time out. Find some time alone, even if only for a few minutes, to collect your thoughts. Recall your goals for your child's character formation. Who do you want your daughter to be when she grows up? How can you apply the rules of good discipline to most effectively help your son become a person of character? Remember, use the least severe methods that will help your child achieve these goals.

If you cannot gain control of your anger, do two things: Call a friend to discuss your situation until you grow calm. And, all the while, talk with the heavenly Father, seeking his ever-ready help in times of trouble (see Ps 46:1). You can conquer any problem with these resources.

Remember, "Train up a child in the way he should go; and when he is old, he will not depart from it" (Prv 22:6). Such training makes children strong—and unlikely to become victims of abuse.

5

Passing on Healthy Attitudes About Sex

One of my fondest childhood memories is Sunday mornings at home just before our family left for church. I would sit in my child-sized rocking chair, dressed in my Sunday best, waiting to hear the church bell toll. I loved the sound of that bell, both for its own sake and because it seemed a signal for Mom and Dad to emerge from their bedroom together. Dressed in their best apparel, they would stop in the little alcove off the dining room, where Dad would put his arms tenderly around my mother. They would look into each other's eyes, and then Dad would gently kiss Mom on the neck. They would smile—and I would know my world was intact. I was safe.

Years later, my daughter told me she felt so good when her dad and I showed affection. And she loved it when she and her brother and sister could break into our hug to form a complete, loving circle. Even our beloved dog would wriggle into that circle when she could!

Generous parent-to-parent and parent-to-child affection teaches healthy attitudes about physical intimacy and helps abuse-proof kids.

Is Your Attitude Healthy?

Wise, informed parents can educate their children about sex, helping them avoid the pitfalls of childish curiosity and adolescent exploitation. To do this, however, parents must have an open, comfortable attitude about sex themselves. They must recognize that the same God who created delicate ears, cute noses, and graceful hands and feet also made the genitals, and that when man and woman were complete, God said, "That's very good" (Gn 1:31).

As a former pediatrician and a mother of three, I know that many parents unwittingly communicate to their children—even babies—an unhealthy attitude about their bodies. I see this when parents change a baby's dirty diapers. Inevitably they make a wry face and say, "Phew!" I doubt it ever occurs to these parents that their distaste teaches their child (yes, even an infant) that the genital area of the body is dirty and bad.

Parents also unknowingly can communicate a negative attitude about the body simply by how they respond when a child touches him- or herself. I've seen mothers call their own mothers long-distance when baby Jill or Jim discovered her ears or his toes. And they take great delight when their babies discover their hands. Indeed, the kaleidoscopic changing of fingers as baby gracefully moves and watches her own hands is fascinating to observe.

But what happens when baby discovers his or her genitalia? I've seen parents slap a baby's hands for exploring this area of the body. This tells the child, "This part of you is bad. Don't touch. Deny that you have sexual parts." This increases the possibility that your toddler will grow to explore his penis (or her clitoris) secretly and perhaps excessively or will try to repress normal, healthy sexuality. Such children may be vulnerable to "exploring parties" with more overt kids. Almost always they will be afraid to ask or to talk about sexual matters with their forbidding parents.

Today's society has conditioned young people to view sex as an exploitive, competitive, and recreational function. Late night talk shows by innuendo and explicit allusions ridicule sex or make it sensational. Even modes of dress and ways of walking have become seriously seductive. Despite—or perhaps because of—this emphasis on sex, parents act embarrassed and give a giddy laugh when I try to discuss sexuality in seminars.

Parents, I urge you to examine your own attitudes. Are you ashamed to discuss sexual issues openly? Do you freeze up and stammer when your child evidences normal curiosity about sexuality? Do you send your child to your spouse or a teacher for answers? Worst of all, do you in any way slam the door against further communication about sex? If so, you need an attitude adjustment.

Here are some things you can do to begin to gain a healthy, biblical, and godly attitude about the human body and sex:

- Review your junior high biology texts. Read about your body from a scientific perspective until you can see it as a marvel of God's creation—not a thing of either shame or ridicule.
- Review the incredibly accurate description of the Creation in Genesis. In just a few words, we have an amazing account of God's perception of us as beings created in his image.
- Talk about sexual issues with your spouse, a friend, or a relative until you lose your uneasiness. Find the terms that are accurate and at least somewhat scientific. It is just as well to discuss your son's penis as his "wiener." Think of the implications of the latter term!
- If you have no one else with whom to practice, talk to

yourself. Use your mirror and discuss the facts, the feelings, and the values you want your child to understand and develop.

- Read *Intimate Issues* by Linda Dillow and Lorraine Pintus (Colorado Springs, Colo.: Waterbrook Press, 1999). Even though this book is written primarily for women, men can also benefit from its insights. The book seeks to educate Christians about God's view of sex and answers many questions that Christian women have surrounding this issue.

Use any means you can, but do develop a wholesome comfort zone about sexual matters. It is important to develop a healthy attitude toward sex in order to teach your child about it and to help prevent him or her from becoming a victim of abuse. It is even more crucial that you develop a broad comfort zone of your own. It is amazing how many fathers and mothers sexually abuse their own children.

Most children are curious about their bodies and may at some time fondle themselves or another child. If you act horrified, ashamed, and embarrassed, your child will not feel comfortable talking with you about these issues and may continue to do them in secret.

Part of having a healthy attitude about sex is recognizing that such curiosity is normal; there is no need to panic. In fact, you can use your child's curiosity to educate him or her further about sex.

What If I Discover My Child Doing Something Sexual?

My friend Florence called me one day in a panic. She had just discovered her five-year-old daughter Lana with her playmate

Nate from next door with their clothes off. They were busily looking at and gently touching each other's genitals. Florence was horrified, but somehow refrained from scolding them until we could talk.

Her story revealed some very useful facts:

- This was the first time such an event had taken place in her child's life;
- The activity was clearly out in the open—there was no excitement from hiding and secrecy attached to the event;
- Neither child was being aggressive with the other;
- Clearly, they were simply curious and innocently trying to discover the differences between boys and girls.

I told Florence to sit down in the shade with both children, share a snack, and have a talk with them. Explain calmly that you understand they were curious, I told her, but that sometimes curiosity can get us in trouble, just like it got Curious George, the monkey in the delightful children's books, in trouble.

I encouraged her to tell them that some things are supposed to be private, including the body parts we cover, so even if a person asks if they can see those body parts, tell them no, and don't let them show theirs, either.

Then, I finished, ask them if they have any questions, and move on to other topics. Read them *Curious George,* or tell a story from your own childhood when you did something impulsive that caused a problem for you.

I warned Florence about stifling the children's truly healthy curiosity, which is a priceless quality that moves us to explore, learn, and grow in knowledge. Yet, like the rest of life, curiosity must be balanced with consideration and caution.

"This sort of innocent curiosity should not create guilt," I said. "Guilt can put a stop to purposefully mean or naughty behavior—which this is not. Be careful to avoid making the kids feel ashamed, but do observe their play more closely. Help them find active, creative projects and games. I predict you'll have no more problems." Fortunately, that was true.

Remember that neglect can be a form of abuse. Had Florence failed to constructively take charge of this situation, both children might have become focused on and fascinated with their sexual selves. Or, had she scolded and shamed them, she could have dumped needless guilt on them with its far-reaching damage. Fortunately, she did neither; she found balance in her approach.

Let me offer one more illustration:

Four-year-old Elsie was enrolled in a clean, light, and colorful preschool. The play areas were well equipped and lovingly supervised. The staff were trained, kind, and seemed to have earned both the love and the respect of the children. Only one area somehow had escaped the careful supervision of the staff—the restrooms.

One day Elsie skipped innocently down the hall to the girls' restroom, where she was surprised to find two other girls with their panties down. They were looking at and touching each other's sexual parts with some intensity. Both of them insisted that she join them in their exciting new play activity. At first, Elsie tried to leave, but the girls, both bigger than she, insisted that she play with them. Finally the little girl joined them briefly, but she was relieved at the approach of footsteps, when the girls hurriedly dressed. No one else saw what had happened.

At that time, Elsie was living with her loving grandparents. She trusted them completely and told her grandmother exactly what had taken place. Her wise grandparents responded well, and did three significant things that helped Elsie.

1. They assured Elsie that they loved her very much and that what had happened was not her fault, but that this sort of play was forbidden. They explained that her body was hers and no one else had the right to "play" with it, nor did she have the right to play with someone else's body. Games and toys are to play with—not children's bodies.

2. They promised to talk with the teachers and make certain that this never happened again. They kindly and clearly instructed Elsie to run to her teacher at once if anyone ever tried to do such a thing again, even if it was with another child.

3. They quietly observed Elsie's conduct with friends, and supervised her closely for some weeks. Finally, they realized she had forgotten the episode and seemed to be restored to her wholesome self.

When sexual encounters in childhood are associated with fear or pain and the child has no confidant, he or she may have sexual problems as an adult. One researcher and author suggests that it is useful for some children not to try to remember abusive experiences.[1] While this theory runs counter to the theories of classical psychiatry, I agree with her.

Teach Your Child to Respect the Human Body

Part of giving your child a healthy attitude about sex means teaching him or her to respect the body. The best way to do that is by example. Tease and tickle only in appropriate ways, not by pinching buttocks or fondling breasts. Never tease a child when he or she asks you to stop or seems uncomfortable.

Play hard, wrestle some, and cuddle, but remember that each part of the human body has a special purpose. Hands are for creating and doing tasks. Mouths are for talking and eating. The genitals are for excretion and ultimately for reproduction. They are not for finding excitement through the exploitation of a child.

Most people were horrified by the recent melee in Central Park in New York City. Some fifty young women were horribly mistreated and sexually abused in full view of the public, and no one came to the rescue of the victims.

A major part of the tragedy lies in the conduct of some of the young women. They were dressed provocatively, and initially they laughed and joined in the "fun." But then the conduct of the young men got out of control. A "mob spirit" surged through the crowd, and tragic atrocities were committed.

Sex is no longer discussed only behind closed doors and in privacy. Television, movies, and talk shows have brought the discussion out in the open. In the sexually charged culture in which we live, parents can help abuse-proof their kids by teaching them what it means to be sexually responsible.

Sexual responsibility means that one never exploits another person for sexual excitement. It means that sex is saved for marital commitment, and that one must show respect in this area to friends and, later, dates.

What else should parents teach their children about sexual responsibility? Here's a list to consider:

- Teach girls to dress respectfully. Parents need to help their daughters understand, before they reach age twelve (puberty), that spaghetti-strap tops and skimpy shorts are "turn-ons" to boys. While dress never justifies sexual assault, part of being "abuse-proof" means dressing wisely. Many attractive styles are not a "turn-on." Wise parents will start early and help their girls dress in cute but not scanty clothes.

- Teach girls to be kind, considerate, friendly, and fun without being seductive. And when your daughter starts dating, she needs a cell phone or pager in case she needs rescuing!
- Teach your sons that they are responsible to protect others, not to exploit them. They are never to push a girl to do sexual things with them. Before they reach puberty, boys need to know that they will be tempted to explore adult ideas and behaviors in the sexual arena, but they must overcome such temptations.
- To discourage your children from trying to act sexy in order to be liked, point out to them how many kids of the opposite sex pay attention to and flirt with them when they are just being themselves. This will help build their self-esteem.
- Teach your children how to recognize and refuse a date's attempts to use them for selfish gratification, which is blatant sexual abuse by peers. Kids must be taught about the incredibly powerful sexual drive that explodes when petting goes too far.
- Keep open the doors of communication about sexual issues. When you feel uneasy about discussions or certain questions your children ask, say so. It's okay to say, "I'm not sure I know the answer to that. I'll look it up and get back to you." Then do that. If your children are too young to understand or cope with certain in-depth concepts, it's okay to say, "That's as complicated

as Greek! Give me time to think about the answer." Just be sure you always get back to them.

- Teach your kids to wait until marriage for sexual intercourse. Teach them that in the marriage union, sex is a wonderful pleasure. Most of us who teach this idea are ridiculed, but experience over time verifies that medically, emotionally, psychologically, and spiritually, postponing sex until after marriage is wise.

Years ago, a young friend told me how he approached every date: "I stand in front of my mirror and I say to myself, 'Steve, you stand in the shoes of Jane's father until you take her home to him.' With that in my mind, I have always been able to resist the strong temptation to get sexual with my date." How I wish every young man thought and acted like Steve!

Just Do It

I know that providing good sex education for your kids is a challenging assignment, one that will take much time, energy, and vigilance on your part. Watch for those golden, teachable moments. Don't be afraid to make mistakes; kids will forgive mistakes. Just be faithful in teaching your children about sex, and especially in teaching the sacred value of sex and the need for respect and dignity toward all sexual issues. Later on, if not now, your children will love you for your efforts.

Parents, you can do it. You can do it best. So do it!

6

Is Your Child Safe at Home and at Play?

With frightening regularity, the nightly news startles us with reports of children being accosted, kidnapped, molested, and even murdered. A few months ago in my city a young girl was attacked in a short underpass that was built to allow children to cross a busy street to and from school. Now the city must find a way to keep children safe in this "safe" walkway!

Parents, it bears repeating: *you* are the most important key in abuse-proofing your children. Being aware of the potential for abuse and being a safe parent who administers healthy discipline and passes on a healthy attitude about sex is only the beginning. To protect your children, you must know them. You must pay attention to what is going on in their lives. To do this, you must know the people who spend time with your child.

Is My Child Likely to Be Victimized?

Research has shown that children who are victimized often have some common personality traits. If you want to abuse-proof your kids, you need to know the following things about them.

1. Is my child's attitude toward his own and others' bodies wholesome? Does he bother playmates or classmates by touching or looking at them too much? Children who have excessive curiosity about bodies may already have experienced some invasion of their own bodies. They need simple instruction about male and female anatomy given calmly, in a manner that satisfies their curiosity without creating even more focus on it.

2. Can my child assert her own rights, but equally give her peers some rights? Teach your child the difference between assertiveness (standing up for fairness for oneself) and aggression (attacking another person). Assertive children have a strong sense of self-worth and can hold their own position about what's right, even when peers disagree. Assertive children know how to say "no" to subtle invitations to do wrong.

Abusers often use aggression—they physically attack another person. Tell your children they should walk away from people who use aggression with them, or ask an adult for help, or scream and run for safety. Teach your children that they are never to attack others except in self-defense.

3. Does my child evidence a sense of caution? Does he approach new people and situations recklessly or stand back and carefully evaluate a new situation before approaching? Some children are born with a greater sense of caution than others. This can be a valuable asset, and you must distinguish it from undue shyness that comes from fear. If your child is so bold that she never knows a stranger, you need to help her develop a healthy reserve around strangers. You can do this by making basic rules for behavior in stores or other public places. "You must stay within my sight [or even by my side]. If we do become separated, find a store clerk who will help you find me." If your child can't or won't follow this rule, you should plan your shopping trips and errands when you have someone with whom to safely leave your child.

You may need to use a tragic news report about a child who strayed or went off with a stranger and came to harm. If you talk about the heartbreaking event in a calm and yet earnest manner, you can usually teach a child the reason for caution.

Some Children Are More Vulnerable

Some children are more vulnerable to abuse simply because of their particular personality traits. Some victims, of course, don't have any of these traits, but most will have one or more. If your child fits any of these descriptions, you might take steps to help him or her combat these traits.

Helplessness. All young children are largely helpless; someone else must meet their every need. Left alone, they will certainly die. Some abused kids tolerate abuse because they are genuinely helpless. They may even go to their abuser for some sort of attention after an episode of abuse.

When an abusive parent repeatedly tells a child, "I only punish you because I love you," the child may become masochistic, perceiving love only through pain. (Sadists, on the other hand, believe the way to show love is to give pain.)

Tragically, sadomasochism has become a fad. Through the Internet and terribly sick newspaper ads, people who associate love with pain find each other. They practice giving and receiving pain, sometimes even to the point of death. If we are ever to stop such evil practices in adults, we must first prevent abuse in childhood, for sado-masochism is born in childhood.

To combat a sense of helplessness in your child:

- Be sure your child learns an appropriate sense of his or her own strength. Strength is the ability to resist stress. It demands durability and comes from learning to do the right thing, even when that's hard and one doesn't want to. Parents cultivate strength in children by requiring them to accomplish challenging tasks and making certain they do their best, thus helping them feel the thrill of achievement.

- Within limits, give your child choices. When parents make too many decisions for a child, he or she will have difficulty knowing how to solve problems and make wise choices for him- or herself. A toddler, for instance, may choose a red or a blue shirt, a big glass of milk or a small one. As your child grows in age and maturity, allow him or her to make more complex choices. Parents must teach wise decision-making so kids can learn to say "No!" to invitations to do wrong.
- Respect your child's feelings. Instead of saying, "We won't tolerate your anger," say, "We understand that you're angry. We all get mad. But let's use that energy to figure out what to do when someone upsets you."
- Find ways to meet your child's needs. Children need unconditional love, pride in and approval of their achievements, reasonable consistency in their lives, and some pleasure and fun. Of course, they need food, clothing, and shelter, too. Meeting these basic *needs* offers security. Parents who provide too many *wants,* on the other hand, can become indulgent, spoiling their child.
- Evidence pride in your child and show unconditional love.
- Never let your growing child believe he or she is helpless; teach your child to find solutions and use them.

Passivity. Children who are vulnerable to abuse typically have less energy than other children. They tolerate much more opposition and show less aggressiveness. They have a lower sensitivity level and respond less intensely to any sort of stimulus. Abusers both consciously and unknowingly take advantage of this by being mean to such children and by overpowering them.

To combat passivity in your child:

- First, be certain that you never bully your child—for instance, with excessive punishment. Simply because you are the parent, when your child hits a sibling you have the power to ground him, spank him, take away his TV time, and demand that he do extra chores. But these measures are extreme for the "crime," and rather than teaching him to be kind to his sibling, they are likely to make him rebellious and mean.
- Teach your child, however passive or reserved, how to stand up to bullies. Children can learn to say, "Don't do (or say) that to me. It hurts my feelings"; or simply, "Don't ever say that to me again." Role playing can teach a child how to be assertive (self-expressive) without being aggressive (attacking). A personal example: My maiden name was Horst, and an annoying boy in my Sunday school class tormented me by calling me "Horsie." I had no idea how to deal with this infuriating peer, so I ignored him. That failed to stop him, so I told my mother how angry I felt at him. She came up with the perfect response. His name was Hornbaker, so she suggested I tell him I'd rather be a horsie than be Steven Bake-the-horn. Teasingly I repeated her exact words. They worked.

- Help your child figure out well-planned responses to attacks from bullies. A carefully planted "give as good as you got" can cure some bullies, as in the example above. Certainly it can help a victim grow into strength instead of remaining in helpless passivity. Take Randy as an example. For a whole semester, a bully in his band class hit Randy's left arm with his knuckles, bruising him terribly. His parents told Randy that if he'd just ignore it, the kid would stop. Yet when the second semester found the bully as abusive as ever, his dad said, "Randy, just look for your chance and try giving one jab back to him." Trust me, Randy loved finding that chance, and when he did, he silently gave back what he'd been getting. To his amazement, he got no more abuse. Obviously, if this were carried too far, Randy could become an abuser himself; but in this particular instance, his response was effective.

Sensitivity. Super-sensitive children often get hurt easily and cry quickly. Abusers often perceive crying as a weakness, and it incites them to more abuse. I have heard and seen an angry parent punish a child and then yell at him for crying about his pain—abuse on top of abuse.

Sensitive victims are not only sensitive to their own pain, they are also sensitive to their perceived abusers. A stern look or a harsh word from a parent or teacher will trigger a flood of tears from one child and be totally ignored by another. You are not necessarily an abuser because your child cries when you correct him or her, but be certain in such cases that you are not being abusive.

It helps to teach sensitive children responses other than

crying. Teach your child the vocabulary of emotions. He can learn to say, "I'm scared and sad because you yelled at me. Please don't yell." Avoid teaching self-pity to a child by over-sympathizing. Help your children discover how to confront bullies firmly and yet courteously rather than accepting abuse as a helpless victim.

One mother taught her sensitive daughter to focus on an angry teacher's heart. "Imagine," Mom said, "that Mrs. Grouch isn't feeling well. Maybe her kids are sick or her husband has been mean to her." Even as a fourth-grader, this gentle girl turned her sensitivity into compassion. She helped change the attitude of the class. Years later, that teacher told the mother how her child had helped her through an extremely difficult year. What a great way to abuse-proof a child: Make of him or her a kind, compassionate, and forgiving person!

Protecting Your Child at Home

As pointed out in the last chapter, the most important thing parents can do to abuse-proof their children is to *give them the protection and nurture they need.* That means creating a loving atmosphere in the home. Also:

- Be sure your children know that it is NEVER acceptable for ANYONE to touch their private parts, and that if someone does, they are to immediately tell you about it.
- Assure your children they can talk to you about *anything*—and then be sure to respond to whatever they tell you with wisdom, grace, and acceptance. Don't judge or react negatively.

If your children feel safe to confide in you, you are much more likely to recognize potential abusers. You will also be able to educate and equip your children to ward off any abuser—even a relative.

How can you know all of the dangerous and potentially dangerous places your children might go? How can you possibly know the people who may harm your child? In today's dangerous world, I believe that parents must assume that any place and any person may put their child at risk. I don't advocate paranoia, but I do strongly encourage you to be responsible for checking out every place your child may go and every person with whom they spend time—even your own family members.

What If You Suspect Your Spouse or Another Relative of Abuse?

How can you know if your spouse or another relative is abusing a child in your home? Here are some warning signs that may indicate abuse:

- A sexually abused child is very likely to act out sexually with other children.
- A sexually abused child often withdraws from normal play activities and becomes preoccupied with sexual fantasies.
- When one child suddenly can do no wrong in the eyes of your spouse, gets special privileges, and acts superior, begin at once to explore the cause. The child's condescension may be covering sadness and guilt.

If you suspect that a child is being abused, don't be afraid to probe for the truth. My favorite motto is, "Explore, don't expect!" By exploring without prejudice, you will usually find the truth—and you may help protect your child from abuse.

If your spouse or another relative is abusing a child and you ignore it, you are adding to the abuse. On the other hand, it's critical that perceived abuse be validated. I know of many families torn apart by false accusations. One parent may accuse the other out of malice; older children may accuse parents in order to manipulate for power or freedom; relatives and even neighbors have reported abuse that never happened. False reports of abuse create havoc in families and inflict injuries that leave scars that last for a lifetime.

If you discover that your spouse or a relative is abusing a child, by law you must report the abuse to the state division of child welfare. Ideally, the state agency will make a fair investigation and find help for the entire family. While this isn't always the case, none of us can risk taking on ourselves the ultimate responsibility for the safety of a helpless child.

If you yourself are the abusive parent, you must get help. Now.

Are Your Children Safe With Each Other?

I receive frantic calls from parents who have discovered that one of their children has sexually molested a brother or sister. Teenagers and young children have told me about dreadful things siblings have done to them. When asked why they didn't report the abuse earlier, some say they were told not to tell and were threatened with death or physical harm if they did. Others say they felt too guilty and ashamed to tell anyone. In such cases, the feelings of fear, guilt, and shame traumatized these kids as much as the incest.

As difficult as this might be for you, as a parent, you need to know that your kids are safe in their own home and in their own beds. Be sure you know what your children are doing when they are alone and playing together.

- Are they too quiet for long periods of time?
- Do they come from playtime looking embarrassed?
- How do they act around each other?
- Does one start to dominate or bully another?

While your kids are playing together, look in on them frequently in a loving, supervisory manner. Avoid suggesting or even implying that they are doing anything inappropriate; this could prompt the very behaviors you want them to avoid. Your gentle intrusion at frequent intervals can prevent various problems and can ensure a safe environment for all of you.

Can You Trust Your Child Sitter?

Be sure you know any and all baby-sitters you have in your homes. Most neighborhood sitters are perfectly wonderful caretakers, but every once in a while we learn of a sitter who has severely abused children under his or her care.

Here are some ways to decrease the likelihood of a child sitter abusing one of your kids:

- Again, be sure that your children know that it is NEVER acceptable for ANYONE to touch their private parts, and that if someone does, they are to immediately tell you about it.
- The first time someone sits for your children, have them do so while you are at home—for instance, when you have guests coming and lots of tasks to do. Use such an occasion to observe how the sitter interacts

with your kids, and above all to observe how your kids react to the sitter.

- As your trust grows, have the sitter watch your kids while you go on a short errand. Return earlier than planned and observe whatever is going on. Pay particular attention to facial expressions, because a sitter who is neglecting or abusing a child usually will look embarrassed or guilty—and so may your kids. Arriving home early also helps you know how responsible the sitter is. My daughter once found her sitter soundly asleep on the sofa while her preschoolers were totally unattended.
- When you plan to be gone for an entire evening, call home unexpectedly. A good sitter, as a rule, will be composed and respectful. Of course, sitters can be terrific actors, so if your children are old enough, be sure to talk with them about what went on while you were gone. Look for any signs of bruising or other hurts.
- If you have serious doubts about the sitter, do not use him or her again.

Don't forget that even a well-known sitter or the child of a good friend can engage in aberrant, impulsive behaviors. That was certainly the case with Jill.

Jill regularly looked after her neighbor's three children. The parents considered her reliable until one day their daughter reported some very inappropriate sex play that the sitter had initiated. The child was embarrassed, but also thought that what had happened was funny. The parents chose to explain to her that this sort of play is not for kids. They told her how proud of her they were for telling them what had happened, but went on to explain that she was never to play this way again. They told her that God made her "private parts" for other purposes.

Then these parents confronted Jill and her parents about what had happened. Jill was indescribably remorseful, and was open and honest about all that had happened. She explained that she had been watching some explicit sexual scenes on a TV show and had impulsively experimented with playing out the scene. Jill never baby-sat for this family again, but she did for other families and became a most responsible and valued sitter.

No matter how well-trained and carefully chosen a sitter is, some maltreatment can happen. If you learn that a sitter has engaged in sexual activity with your child, do as these parents did. Talk to the sitter and his or her family about what has happened, so that the sitter can receive help. And then find a new sitter.[1]

The Internet and TV

With the recent advances in technology, strangers and abusive material now have unprecedented access into our homes, particularly through the Internet and cable television. This has opened up a new avenue of potential harm for kids.

In their own homes, at school, in public libraries, and in the homes of friends, most of America's children and youth have access to atrocious knowledge. Through e-mail, chat rooms, and long-distance phone calls, pornography and evil of monstrous proportions are instantly available.

Recently someone in my city found five barrels in a barn in a rural area. The barrels contained the bodies of women and at least one child. The owner of the property is accused of killing these people, one by one. In every case, the initial contact was made over the Internet.

Parents, supervise your children's use of the Internet. *Do not practice the abuse of neglect.* It's your job to monitor technology in your home. Teach your child what makes something wrong. I have come up with the following criteria, which I encourage you to talk over with your children:

1. An act is wrong if it lessens your potential for good—morally, intellectually, or spiritually, as well as physically. For example, smoking, using drugs, and abusing alcohol damage your body. Inflicting bodily injury or hurting others' feelings damages them as well as your own conscience. Don't do anything that causes harm to yourself or others.

2. An act is wrong if it diminishes your future opportunities. For instance, certain kinds of computer games that teach violent behavior can lead to actions that may result in jail time. Refusing to study and blowing off your responsibilities can lessen your chances of getting into a good college, which might put career opportunities at risk. Relying too much on computers can make your brain lazy; you need to learn to *think* as well as master the use of technology.

3. An act is wrong if it hurts or puts down people around you. Under no circumstances, not even in TV cartoon programs, is it okay for one human being to bully, attack, diminish, or in any way hurt another.

4. An act is wrong if it goes against the commands of God in his Word. God's laws are distinctly made for our good. To go against them can only be wrong.

You may come up with other criteria to help your children identify right from wrong. Be sure they are valid, and then teach them. In addition to the above guidelines, I encouraged my children to ask themselves: If everyone in the world did this act, would the planet be a better place or not?

Here are some additional things you should do to abuse-proof your child against technology:

- Use the available locks to delete pornographic materials from your TV and computer screens.
- Keep TVs, telephones, and computers out of your children's bedrooms; these items isolate your kids from you. Individual rooms are for sleep, study, and periods of privacy. When electronic devices are kept in common family areas, you can see and hear what your child is seeing and hearing, and you have the opportunity to teach the basic values you want to pass on.
- Set specific limits on your children's use of the Internet. Establish time limits. Encourage older kids to be discerning about how they use the Internet and to set their own boundaries.
- Watch the programs your kids are watching on TV. Guide them to see what's abusive in even the cartoons they watch. Your guidance not only helps abuse-proof your children, it teaches them to recognize their own abusive behavior.
- Teach your kids the true loveliness of sexual intimacy as God designed it to be. Sex as created and blessed by God is one of the greatest gifts he has given human beings, but stained by distortions of its best expression between husband and wife, it can become a curse of the worst sort. Protect your children from this curse.

Protecting Your Child in Public Places

Here are some things you can do to help your children remain safe when they are in public places:

- Teach caution without inciting fear. If you are taking a kindergartner or preschooler shopping with you, explain that he or she must stay with you all the time. Give your child a reason: sometimes children get lost, and another person who wants a child could take him or her away. Be sure that your child follows this rule. If he or she does stray, make sure there is a consequence, such as cutting short the shopping trip.
- Tell your kids to NEVER
  1) go *anywhere* with a stranger.
  2) take anything from a stranger.
  3) allow a stranger to touch them.
- Tell them to ALWAYS
  1) stay some distance away from strangers. (Show them what that means.)
  2) avoid playing or walking in areas where no one else is around. Before a child agrees to help a man near the neighborhood shopping center, for example, he or she should look around to see if other people are nearby. Better yet, he or she can offer to get another adult to help.
  3) call for help and run away if they sense danger. In a dangerous situation, it's usually safer to have your child seek protection from a woman than from a man. Most women do have a mothering instinct that keeps them from hurting a child.

- Role play with your children to teach them how to respond in potentially dangerous situations. First, have them take the dangerous-stranger role while you play the child. They'll gain profound insights as they enter, in their imaginations, this dark side of the adult world. Then reverse roles and let them practice their skills at identifying and evading a risky situation.
- Teach your children how to read faces by having them draw sketches of kind, angry, sly, or threatening facial expressions. Educate them about signs of danger. A touch, a smirk, certain kinds of eye contact, being followed by a stranger are all signs that it's time to walk rapidly away toward a safe-looking adult.
- Encourage your children to trust their feelings about people. Tell them that if they feel like avoiding or running from someone, that's exactly what they should do.
- Be certain you know the families of your children's friends and playmates. When your child visits the home of a neighbor, friend, or business associate, ask him or her what they did while they were alone together. Look for signs of embarrassment or discomfort. Invite your child's confidence and be sure he or she feels that it is safe to tell you things.
- As long as your children are comfortable with you doing so, accompany them when they are being examined physically by a doctor. When they ask you to stop accompanying them, educate them about what to expect from the exam or visit, and remind them about what is inappropriate behavior from a medical or dental professional. Talk with them after the appointment

and ask them if they felt comfortable with how they were treated.

- Always go with your kids when they play in a public park. Unfortunately, many parks are no longer safe places for children to play alone.
- Don't let your children walk or ride a bike alone. Check out all the places where your children might walk or ride their bikes. Make certain that any unpaved trails are open and have good visibility. Instruct your children to look around as they ride; tell them if anyone follows or approaches them to instantly and quickly go to a busy street or a place where there are other people.
- Provide a pager or portable phone to your pre- and early adolescent children to use in case of emergencies. The years when your children are growing toward independence and are more likely to be free from adult supervision are their most vulnerable.
- Pray for your child's safety. Yes, bad things happen even when parents pray. On the other hand, we may never know how often God's invisible angels have protected our children from danger.

7

Is Your Child Safe at School?

Mrs. Jones had two exceptionally bright girls in her fifth-grade class. Intending only to motivate them to excellence, she set them at odds through extremely competitive assignments. Before long, the two girls hated each other—and never understood that their teacher had hurt them both by setting up the competition.

Eight-year-old David saw a film at school about stranger abuse that depicted terrifying stories. For a long while afterward, he suffered nightmares and grew fearful of most people. His wise parents were finally able to help him recover from his fears, but his case helps us realize that schools must observe precautions or the "cure" for abuse may itself become abusive.

One teacher I know punished a student for breaking a rule by writing her name on the blackboard and then making her sit in the small cubbyhole beneath her desk. Another gives children a yellow card for minor offenses like forgetting to put their name on a paper. When a child gets three yellow cards, he or she has to walk back and forth on a yellow line in the playground. During the entire recess period, the children thus punished become objects of shame and ridicule to the other kids.

These are all examples of the sorts of abuse your child may suffer at school. Teachers, aides, coaches, janitors, cooks, fellow students, and principals have been known to abuse school children emotionally, socially, intellectually, and sexually. Strangers, too, can victimize school children by luring them away from the playground or from their routes to and from school.

Our schools have been entrusted with the role of protecting, guiding, and teaching appropriate life skills to our young people, but unfortunately, we can no longer assume that our children are safe from abuse because they are in a classroom. The ultimate responsibility for your child's safety still resides with you. The key is to *make it your business to know your children's schools.*

Get Involved!

I always urge parents to get involved at their children's schools. I especially encourage them to know how the school addresses potential dangers that students might encounter.

Many children see violence on TV or read about it in comic books on a regular basis. Many also face danger daily right in their own neighborhoods. We don't expect them to encounter images of violence in school; yet the way some schools present information to students about danger from strangers can be as terrifying as anything they will ever encounter. Perhaps more so, because this sort of real danger impacts children directly.

Parents need to be involved in deciding how their child's school presents information about "stranger danger." Gather together a group of parents to brainstorm ideas about how to inform and safeguard your children without terrifying them. Since most schools educate students about the danger of strangers through the use of films, I recommend you consider the following questions as you brainstorm:

1. How old are the children? What is the best way to present this kind of material to children of this age? Younger children (up to seven) may need to have a more gentle presentation of the potential for danger than what a graphic film affords. For example, a teacher or a parent volunteer might help students create skits in which the children take turns playing the roles of a suspicious stranger or an aggressive older kid, learning in the process how to act, when to run, and how to call for help in such a situation.

Advice to students should always be definite and clear: "Don't ever go anywhere with someone you don't know." "Always tell a teacher if a stranger comes near you or tries to talk to you or another student." "Yell and run fast if you feel afraid of a stranger." I recommend that parents of young children teach these directives at home as well.

2. Are there children in the classroom who are particularly sensitive of spirit? This may be difficult to ascertain because by school age, many kids have learned to hide their feelings. But any child who evidences a super-sensitive or fearful type of personality may need special treatment in this area. Parents know their child better than anyone and need to communicate this knowledge to their child's teacher appropriately.

3. Will parents be invited to be a part of this educational focus? Before the school shows a film to its students about this topic, parents should be invited to see it, take part in discussions, and help decide how and to whom it will be presented. Obviously parents will disagree on many points, and certainly everyone can't be pleased, but if every parent's ideas are heard, many fewer mistakes will transpire.

4. Will there be any follow-up after the presentation? After a presentation of this nature, students of all ages should be encouraged to discuss the topic in small groups. Remember, the more actively children are involved in learning, the better the lesson sticks in their minds. I recommend that parents ask to be included in the follow-up in some way. A discussion for parents alone or for parents and children together can set the stage for further healthy instruction at home about the potential danger of strangers. A related possibility for follow-up is for a skilled counselor to help children and parents present a skit depicting good family discussions.

Once you've come up with a list of good ideas to help educate your children about "stranger danger," present them to your school principal or to the district superintendent and school board. Participating in abuse-prevention programs at school enables parents to reinforce vital information at home.

What Parents and Schools Must Teach

To begin with, schools must have some awareness of what is appropriate and inappropriate in relations between a child and an adult. Even more, they must assume some responsibility for maintaining a safe environment at school and for teaching students to recognize and avoid danger. If your school isn't currently doing this, your involvement can help make it happen.

Instruction to help children avoid danger should always include the following principles:

1. *Our world is not always a safe place.* Sex offenders hang around playgrounds and abduct and hurt children. If children know this they will be at least a little more alert and cautious.

2. *Trust your instincts about danger.* Teachers can show children photographs to help them identify facial expressions of angry people, but they should also tell them that many dangerous people can look like an uncle or a grandfather. Kids

need to know that even if a person looks friendly, if they sense danger, they need to trust their intuition and avoid that person.

3. Never do what a stranger asks of you. Never go anywhere with a stranger. I've already emphasized that parents must keep preschoolers and even early school-aged children within their sight and hearing in public places. But, I repeat, if your child can't or won't stick to you like glue when you're away from home, do not take him or her with you. You, the parent, must determine *any* exceptions to this rule.

4. If a stranger tries to grab or touch you, scream loudly, fight hard, and if you can, run fast.

5. There is such a thing as good touch and there is such a thing as bad touch. In preschools all over the country, efforts are being made to distinguish good from bad touch. Be sure your child knows the difference between the two:

Good touch is calming and comforting. It is a pat or a stroke on the head. It is a pat on the back, or an arm around the shoulder. It makes the recipient feel safe and warm. It's never below the waist. Bad touch often feels "slimy." It is aimed at, or works its way toward, the breasts, buttocks, or genitals—the "private parts."

Teach your child to never tolerate bad touch. They have to know that sometimes bad touch will be attempted not by strangers but by other children or even by people they know. It's never okay to allow this sort of touch. To protect themselves and other kids who might be too shy to tell, they must report to a teacher and parent anyone who ever tries to touch them in a bad way. Assure them that this is not tattling; it's preventing harm.

6. You must never try to give anyone a bad touch. Tell children that if they feel like doing so, or if they are curious about the private parts of their body, they should talk to their parents and their teacher, who can help them control their behavior and stay out of big trouble, as well as teach them the good facts about the whole body.

7. *Never try to show off your body.* Teach children that they should never show another child their private parts. Doing so makes others uncomfortable and will get them in trouble.

8. *Don't focus your mind on bodies and the excitement that thinking about them sometimes arouses.* Let children know that their job now is to be a good student, a fine athlete, a caring friend, and a good person.

With appropriate vocabulary, these principles can readily be adapted to any grade level. If every parent and teacher taught them and every child learned them well, in time we could transform our entire sex-obsessed culture. In any case, they should be essential components in our efforts to abuse-proof our children.

Identifying Intellectual Abuse

Teachers more commonly engage in emotional and intellectual abuse than sexual abuse. Teachers often feel overwhelmed, and their personal lives may add even more stress to their jobs. Blatant abuse is not too difficult to recognize, but there are subtle ways in which both teachers and parents may intellectually abuse children. Here are some things to watch for:

1. *Undue competition.* Let me hasten to say that good competition can be a motivator. It's fun and exciting. But watch your child's teacher lest she carries competition too far. And never cross that line with your own children at home.

2. *Destroying a child's self-confidence.* Granted, some conformity

is necessary for any school, but let me tell you about Brent, my grandson. He's a quiet and sensitive child who thinks a lot and tries hard to do the right thing. Early in the year, his third-grade teacher ridiculed him in front of the entire class for his particular way of laughing. He turned red, felt shame he could only barely describe to his mother, and somehow refrained from ever laughing again in that class. His wise parents encouraged laughter at home, reassured him this was his teacher's problem, and helped him maintain self-respect. But that teacher abused Brent. I hope his mom's letter to the teacher helped prevent her from ever repeating such a cruel action.

Teachers abuse children daily by ignoring them, shaming them in front of their peers, and failing to recognize their nonacademic gifts. Parents need to make such teachers aware of their mistakes and offer better ideas for motivating kids.

Preventing Emotional Abuse

Emotional abuse by authority figures and peers occurs all too frequently in school classrooms, on school grounds, and on sports fields.

A kindergartner, Frank sometimes sucked his thumb. His teacher, believing she had to break him of this habit, made this sensitive little boy stand up in front of his entire class and suck his thumb. She invited his classmates to make fun of him. The same teacher locked another student in a dark closet because he was restless. An older student found him there an hour later. He had cried himself to sleep. Fortunately, this teacher lost her job because of her abusive actions.

In order to be sure that your child isn't exposed to emotional abuse, get to know your child's teacher. Explore his or her teaching methods carefully. Visit the classroom regularly and, by all means, speak up loudly when you discover abuse. Frank's teacher clearly abused her students under the guise of teaching them childhood social skills. Remember, abuse can be defined as any misuse, hurting, or insulting language that leaves a child's body or emotions permanently damaged.

Kids, too, can be emotionally abusive to one another. Boys who are bullies may physically or verbally abuse a "weaker" boy after school. Girls often form cliques and then exclude other girls from their group, making cutting remarks about how the "outsiders" look or act. Such abuse has long-lasting ramifications on the child's self-esteem—especially if the child's parents aren't proactively instilling a strong sense of self in the child.

Not long ago my niece observed a child at her son's school hitting and yelling at another boy. She could have considered it none of her business, but she knew the lasting scars of such abuse and went to bat for the child. In a few weeks that school was no longer tolerating bullying behaviors. You can make a difference!

What If Your Child Is Abused at School?

If your child has been ill-treated by a teacher, comfort that child and rebuild his or her self-esteem to prevent the abuse from scarring him or her for life. Then address the issue at school, making sure that in your efforts to effect change, you don't abuse the teacher:

1. Report the abuse to the teacher and the principal. Define clearly what kind of abuse is happening. Intellectual abuse is not uncommon in today's agnostic world. A teacher who ridicules a student who believes in creationism instead of evolution can hurt that student emotionally, and can also create doubts in a child's mind about his intelligence, his parents' teachings, and his faith. Making an agnostic out of a child of faith becomes an issue for eternity. Our constitution supports religious freedom, and no one has a right to rob a child of faith.

If the teacher is emotionally abusing the child through harsh discipline:

- Talk with the teacher, telling her what kind of correction you have found works with your child.
- Find out what your child is doing that causes trouble in the classroom and try to correct that behavior at home.
- If the teacher does not improve, talk with the principal. Try not to whine; instead, present clear examples that demonstrate the abuse. If you can get other parents with similar experiences to accompany you, the confrontation will be more effective.

2. *Ask for specific changes and follow through to make sure that they occur and last.* Sometimes schools tolerate teacher abuse. It's hard to prove; teachers' unions tend to protect teachers and not kids; and school administrators are terrified of lawsuits. You will need to be persistent and courageous. Be sure of the truth and avoid being paranoid or picky. Seek the opinions and help of other staff and parents. But don't tolerate teacher abuse.

3. *If the administrator does not effect a change, remove your child from the school.* I urge you in such a case, if you can possibly afford it, to place your child in a private school. If that is truly not possible, you may greatly benefit your child by homeschooling. We now have college students who are living proof that homeschooling is excellent education.

4. *If your child is resilient and the abuse is not horrible, coach him or her about how to behave so as to avoid most of the cruelty.* Use the situation as an opportunity to teach your child how to cope with a difficult person.

Schools are beginning to realize the risks to children from their own staff members, from teachers and principals to library aides and maintenance personnel. Preemployment checks are becoming more stringent. Many states now require paroled sex offenders to register their whereabouts, and schools and other organizations serving children have this information made available to them. There are also psychological tests that help determine a tendency toward abuse by a potential employee.

School administrators, as well as the school staff, must remain alert to the possible intrusion of peer abuse into their classrooms. When a major example of peer abuse occurs, like the shootings in Columbine High School in Colorado, or when a teacher rapes or seduces a student, every school in the nation goes on "red alert." But only for a while. Until another startling event occurs, people gradually and naturally tend to forget.

I spent twenty years working with schools as a result of one caring principal who felt that he alone could not cope with the intimidation caused by several groups of students in his building. He asked me to help him teach a series of classes for all his teachers about how to work with these abusive children. The teachers learned how to set limits and establish effective consequences when a student broke through those boundaries. We did the same with the parents of the kids in the school, and in a year's time, we had transformed not only the school but the community as well.

If your child is being intimidated or ridiculed by other

students, get your parent-teacher association organized and focused. Don't go in with only a complaint; put together some common-sense ideas to make things better.

Helping Teachers Helps Prevent Abuse

As parents, you cannot afford to forget that teachers these days are often overwhelmed in their jobs. They are under pressure to bring up their students' achievement scores. They must cope daily with kids who actively resist learning, show disrespect, and may erupt violently at the least provocation.

Volunteer to help your children's teachers. As you relieve some of their pressures, they can be more watchful for abuse and, perhaps, more patient and encouraging to their students. When you are in your child's school, be alert. Listen to conversations and observe interactions at all levels. Try to get a feel for the emotional climate. If it's lacking the warmth and comfort children need to thrive, do something.

Over the years, teachers have given me a number of ideas about ways parents can help them significantly improve their performance. Here's a sampling:

1. *Write your child's teachers short notes thanking them for their hard work.* This can do more to prevent teacher-to-student abuse than an edict from the school board.

2. *Offer to help grade papers or type a new test.* Many schools benefit greatly from help of this sort that frees a teacher to teach.

3. *If you are able, offer to tutor a needy child in his or her most difficult subjects.* Many kids' parents can't help them with the homework that is so crucial to academic success. In the elementary school my grandsons attend, a corps of dedicated grandparents volunteer to drill children with math flash cards, to review spelling lists, or simply to read to them.

4. Help organize a volunteer program in your school. Remember to screen and supervise the volunteers to avoid anyone who might be yet another abuser. Get together a small group of parents to help you plan such a program, get permission to do it, and then supervise and maintain it. If your own child's school does not need such a service, look for one that does. There are many, especially in larger towns and cities.

5. On a regular basis offer treats in the staff lounge. During my years as consultant to a school district in my city, I learned to schedule my Friday mornings to be at Smith-Hale Middle School. The staff lounge was always loaded with fruits, cookies, and veggies with dip. The school's parent support group unfailingly provided these treats for the staff—a good send-off for a good weekend.

6. When you observe significant problems in your school, come up with some ideas for solving them. Neither teachers nor administrators want to hear whining. They hear plenty of that already. But if you and a few other positive-thinking parents will, you can formulate some creative answers that will help the entire school. Communicate these ideas to appropriate authorities along with an offer to help in any way possible. I have done a lot of such work. Not all of my ideas were accepted, but a surprising number were—and they made a difference. So can yours.

7. Run for school board membership. Many times Christians, who have the most solid values and are connected to God's own power, are afraid to enter the arena of politics. I know political games are often ugly, even dirty. But with good support and heroic effort, you have as good a chance as anyone. You must, of course, have some specific goals and the courage to defend them.

Yes, running for office and serving on the school board take the commitment of considerable time and money. And when no one else on the board agrees with you, it may be lonely and hard to go it alone. Yet you won't really be alone. God and those who support you will be there for you—or at least God will be! Our public schools everywhere have immense needs. For many reasons, we all must pitch in and help.

Protection to and From School

Most schools train older students to serve as school crossing guards; these students learn the rules of behavior and safety that protect all students. If your school offers this valuable service, teach your children to respect these student helpers. If not, once again I urge you to get other parents to help you organize a school safety patrol.

Many schools, especially in large cities, hire adults to stand watch in busy traffic areas. These uniformed people not only protect kids from traffic hazards, they are also alert to dangers of abuse or abduction by strangers. Parents who volunteer regular time to patrol a school area offer additional safety to children.

Kids don't have to attend Sunday school. There's no requirement that children join Scouts or attend community groups to improve their lives. But every child is required by law to attend school. It's in and through our schools that every child can be touched for good. Investing generously of your resources in your local schools is one of the most important ways you can help abuse-proof your children—and perhaps other children not as fortunate as your own.

Preventing Sexual Abuse at School

We've all heard the tragic story of the female teacher who had a sexual relationship with a young teenaged boy and became pregnant by him. She is now in prison for her crime of sexual abuse. News stories from around the country reveal other incidents of sexual exploitation of students by school staff, from principals to maintenance workers. Just last year some five or six school employees in my city—both men and women—were found guilty of sexual involvement with junior and senior high school students. More rarely, elementary school kids are also molested by teachers.

In addition, students sometimes sexually explore or molest other children. Why? Sexually explicit material arouses sexual feelings in most children, even those as young as four or five. Because they don't know how to comprehend or express these intense feelings, they sometimes act out what they've seen—or what they've experienced—on their peers. Whether they are exploring or maliciously molesting the other child is irrelevant. In either case, the victim is equally devastated. Many schools now have restroom supervisors to ensure that restrooms are safe for kids to use, but that alone isn't enough.

While our schools have been entrusted with the role of protecting, guiding, and teaching appropriate living to our young people, the ultimate responsibility resides with parents. Get involved with your child's school. Know your child's teachers. If your child relays information about sexual improprieties, tell a counselor or teacher. Again, offer suggestions and volunteer time to help if the school wants or needs it.

Remind your child that if *anyone*—whether a teacher, janitor, principal, aide, fellow student, security guard, or coach—says or does something that makes your child feel uncomfortable, he or she needs to tell you about it immediately. If your child accuses someone of impropriety, check it out. Do know your child, and be sure he or she isn't falsely reporting someone he or she may be angry with.

Sadly, it is a child's all-too-brief period of innocence—something that can never be regained—that is lost through sexual abuse. With parental help, the experience can be integrated into the child's fund of knowledge, and he can learn from the trauma and move on—sometimes with no demonstrable harm. Nevertheless, preventing abuse of this kind in our schools must be a priority.

In summary, make it your business to know about your children's schools. Affirm their strengths. Confront their problems politely. Offer ideas for solutions. Give your time and energy both to help and to recruit help.

You can make a difference.

8

Is Your Child Safe at Church?

While growing up, I heard countless sermons on punishment and hell. There were many nights I couldn't sleep because I was afraid I would wake up in hell. I fully believed that if I wasn't perfect, I would go straight to hell if I died. And since I knew I wasn't perfect, when I prayed, "If I should die before I wake, I pray thee, Lord, my soul to take," I meant it. Only I feared that he wouldn't take me because of my sins!

I also heard Satan described as "a roaring lion, seeking whom he might devour" (1 Pt 5:8). Because my young mind could think only concretely, I saw him that way: roaring, coming after me, wanting to eat me up. Such images terrified me and kept me awake many nights. In my private practice of psychiatry, I have encountered children who evidence the same sort of terror I knew.

Many children are highly sensitive and susceptible to the fear tactics that some Sunday school teachers (and parents) use in their eagerness to see children come to Jesus. While the strategy may bring children trembling to Jesus, it doesn't afford them rest in his loving, strong, and protective arms. I find that tragic. Teachers who use these tactics often have the best of intentions, but their failure to present the whole biblical picture keeps children from growing up in their faith; fear consumes them, and the frightening images can haunt them for years.

Don't get me wrong. I have no doubt that evil and Satan exist—I wouldn't be writing this book otherwise. I also have no doubt there is a hell that was made for the devil and his evil angels. But when children are constantly threatened with hell and eternal punishment, they receive an unbalanced and inaccurate picture of biblical truth.

Yes, Christ died in order to defeat Satan and overcome evil. But through Christ we also have the promise of eternal life. Furthermore, the God I serve is one who will exert every influence to guide his children in life and, after death, take them to heaven. I'm certain he's not trying to catch us in an error so he can send us to hell.

Parents, if your church primarily uses fear tactics like the ones I've described, be aware that your children are being subjected to spiritual abuse. Here are some things you can do to protect them:

- Pray daily with your child, thanking God for his promises of love and protection.
- Teach your child the gospel of redemption, not the terrifying one of abrupt, harsh, vengeful punishment.
- Prayerfully consider attending a church that is not spiritually abusive.
- Read Bible stories to your children as well as some of the good, Christian, Bible-based fiction that clearly depicts God's love and redemption.

Fear tactics aren't the only form of spiritual abuse. Rigidity, gossip, and other judgmental attitudes and behaviors are also abusive. Children who don't have "star" quality can be neglected in a Sunday school or youth group setting. Tragically, sexual molestation also occurs within church communities.

Excessive Rigidity

My youngest was an especially tenderhearted child. She loved Jesus and almost everyone else. One Sunday her Sunday school teacher approached me with grave concern about this child. "Wendy never closes her eyes when we pray. She just looks around and even looks out the window!"

Curious to know why this woman was so horrified, I asked, "Does Wendy take part in the prayers? Is she reverent?"

"Oh, she does take part, all right, but I just think she's terribly irreverent when she won't even close her eyes during prayers!"

I do not believe this teacher should have been working with children—she oozed condemnation. I'm certain my child felt this condemnation, and others must have felt it as well. I can find no place in the Bible where we're told to close our eyes to pray. I suspect that Wendy, like I do, saw God in his creation outside that window. I don't believe she saw him in her teacher.

Rigid church doctrine can also result in spiritual abuse. For example, many denominations teach that babies must be baptized to gain eternal life. Others believe that baptism brings salvation to adults. Still others believe it is right to baptize a child only after he or she accepts Christ as Savior. When a church—like the one in which I grew up—teaches that people who don't accept their specific doctrine cannot make it to heaven, many people are left out. Children can be deeply wounded when they are led to believe that their dear friends who attend "that" church may never go to heaven. Such judgment and criticism are basically abusive.

Teach your kids that the Bible tells us we are not to judge. Teach them that God is loving and merciful, and that his Spirit will reveal necessary truth to those who love him. Tell them that even true believers simply can't see every issue exactly alike, and that outside the confines of simple, biblical truth, we should practice tolerance of beliefs that are different from our own.

Abuse by Neglect

In any children's group, a few kids stand out due to their appearance, personality, or mannerisms. These "stars" are selected for the big performance role in Sunday school and church productions. Yet what about less talented children? They would benefit the most if they got, even occasionally, a leading role. I have often looked at the downcast faces of children who are consistently overlooked for significant parts in special performances.

Parents, once again, you are the ones who must speak up. Don't be defensive, and don't do anything until your anger simmers down. But then speak to your pastor or the children's minister and suggest a more fair plan of taking turns so that every child gets a chance to be the star. Work with your child so that when she does get to perform, she does her very best.

If your church leaders don't get the point and don't open up opportunities to all the kids, you are left with helping your own child overcome the sadness of feeling left out. Here are some ways to do that:

- Compliment your child on the good qualities he or she evidences in church (and home) activities.
- Teach your child God's unconditional love, especially for children, and demonstrate such love yourself.
- Any child can be kind and thoughtful to peers. Teach your child that showing these qualities is far more important in God's eyes than being the biggest star ever!

- If your child *is* the star, help him or her avoid acting superior or arrogant. Explain to your child that special abilities are gifts from God. We should be grateful for them, but never "stuck-up" or arrogant.

"You're Bad!"

Most groups have ornery kids who get into trouble—or cause it. More often than not, even in churches, teachers punish such children. Even worse, the "good" kids shun them. Parents often refuse to let their children play with "bad" kids. Obviously, in most cases, this treatment makes these troubled kids even worse. The scars on their hearts last a lifetime.

Some ideas to help *you* help the troubled kids in your church:

- Pray for them and ask God to show you how Jesus Christ would treat them. I believe he would recognize that naughty children often have been hurt by abuse. He would comfort their pain, then teach them right behaviors.
- Teachers might, in love, keep a "problem" child near them. A touch or a warning glance will often ward off a negative behavior.
- Invite these children into your own home. Teach a misbehaving child logical and fair boundaries. Help your children to show this child how to have great fun without misbehaving. This takes time and effort, but it can help change the child's entire life.
- Either a teacher or a parent might go to the parent of a troubled child and kindly offer a description of a particular behavior problem and help in solving it. Granted, the parent may refuse help and even deny the problem, but you will at least have offered assistance.

If churches do not recognize and help fulfill the needs of kids, who will? Parents and children's workers, you *are* the church. Use your opportunities there to offer healing through love and the building up of self-worth. Help abuse-proof all the children in your sphere of influence.

Sexual Molestation

Churches offer wonderful opportunities for those who love God and people and who have talents for serving as volunteers. Working with babies in a nursery, toddlers in a care center, children in Sunday school, or adolescents in a youth program can have a lifelong impact for good. I still remember my kindergarten Sunday school teacher. Her creative ideas made Bible stories come alive for me.

I wish all those who worked in the church had this woman's kind heart and nurturing ways. Sadly, that isn't the case. Youth leaders, Sunday school teachers, and the clergy sometimes engage in sexual abuse, doing great harm to the children placed in their safekeeping. These people, by virtue of their positions in the church, promise to be protectors, mentors, and friends to children; when they violate that trust, they rob kids of their innocence and often of their faith.

Documentaries on TV tell the stories of priests who, over periods of years, molested the students who were entrusted to their spiritual care. Rampant sexual abuse has been uncovered in more than one religious boarding school. For years, sometimes in response to threats, the truth about such abuse lay hidden with its victims. Allegations were disregarded as lies. Weren't these teachers men of God? They wouldn't do such acts. Yet eventually the ugly truth came out.

I've heard many other heartbreaking stories. One involved a male volunteer who took his Sunday school class of preteen girls swimming. He offered to play with them, but his "play" included touching the girls in highly sensitive areas. Somehow he made it seem okay, even exciting and fun. Fortunately, one of the girls realized how wrong it was and told on him.

Then there's the story of Debbie, a thirteen-year-old girl who struggled with self-confidence. With no gifts in music or drama, she missed out on any chance to be a "star" in her church or to gain in any other way the attention and admiration she so needed. Gradually, her youth pastor enticed her into his web, seducing her and using her sexually over a period of months; he stopped only when he left the church for another youth pastor position. How many more needy adolescents did this man destroy? One can only wonder.

What Can Parents Do?

Sadly, people who truly love God sometimes do terribly wrong things. No doubt they have been abused themselves, and the old scars they bear fester into seemingly uncontrollable impulses to act out their abuse on others. To protect your children from sexual abuse at the hands of church workers, I recommend the following:

- Again, be sure that your child knows that it is NEVER acceptable for ANYONE to touch their private parts, and that if someone does, the child is to immediately tell you about it.
- Become well acquainted with your church staff. Invite them into your home, observe them carefully, and if

what you see suggests the possibility of abuse, speak up.
- If you have reasons to be suspicious, remember: explore, but don't expect. In order to be fair, to be accurate, and to avoid getting downright paranoid, seek input from other parents or from a professional counselor.
- Find someone who knows about sexual abuse and who is able to help you take action if you find it is needed.

It's always better to raise questions about a potential abuser than to find out later about damage that can never be undone. Do remember, however, to do in love whatever you decide must be done. Tough love is nonetheless love.

How Can Servants of God Abuse?

A word of caution: Sometimes accusations of sexual abuse are false and malicious. Other times, people in therapy have what is called "false memory retrievals" called up by well-meaning therapists who are searching for possible explanations for clients' symptoms. Most of the therapists I know practice great caution to avoid stirring up such imagined false events, but it can happen.

Certainly severely abused victims may deeply repress (hide in their subconscious mind) abusive episodes from their past. Yet most of my abused patients have vivid memories of their abuse. When they decide they can trust me, they describe the abuse and their abuser in great detail. Fortunately, relating those painful events to a safe person promotes healing.

Over many years I've pondered how and why people who profess to love and serve God can be abusers. Here are my thoughts:

1. Some are outright dishonest. These wolves in sheep's clothing may enter Christian service to relieve their guilt, but more likely because the church is a rich source of victims. They learn to act righteously and become good at convincing others they are godly men and women.

2. *Some feel that Christian work will counteract their base desires.* They hope that biblical truth and God's power will protect them from themselves, even though they have told no one of their struggle and have not reached out for help. They convince themselves they are really okay when in truth they are not. As the prophet said, "The heart is deceitful above all things, and desperately wicked: who can know it?" (Jer 17:9).

3. *Some use their job as a cover-up.* A physician friend told me that abusers follow a definable trail to their abuse episodes. The desire to sexually abuse starts with a need, such as power, warmth, or sex. The need leads to a fantasy, often a vivid one that is played and replayed in the person's mind. The fantasy becomes more and more real and includes a step-by-step plan for *making* it real. At last, the offender decides to act out the picture in his or her mind—and does so. In the case of a church worker who follows this progression, the job serves as a cover-up.

4. *Some have lost the will or the ability to discern right from wrong and the truth from the lie.* Some years ago, I read a book about the Nazi doctors who practiced medicine in World War II. Part of the time they were superbly trained, compassionate physicians, loving husbands, and playful fathers. But then they served in concentration camps where they made guinea pigs out of people, depriving them of even basic medical care and often torturing them. Somehow, in the next hour they could return to being great humanitarians. Denying the truth and rationalizing in order to make wrongs seem right, these men were truly two different persons in one body. The psychological term for the phenomenon is "splitting."

The Creator gave an amazing gift to humankind—the power to choose. I believe God's Spirit reveals truth to us but never forces us to follow it; practicing obedience is a matter of our own free will.

The church has at its disposal the source of all truth. We must use that truth both to set the sinner free from the power of his sin and to protect his potential victims.

How Can the Church Help?

Churches, through the efforts of self-sacrificing, godly men and women, accomplish far more good than evil. Church workers are often poorly paid and overworked, and many volunteers are paid not a penny. In order to help make your church a safe place for your child—and other children—encourage church leaders to do the following:

1. *Select staff carefully.* Excellent screening tests to help find psychologically healthy people are available. A widely used test is the M.M.P.I. (Minnesota Multiphasic Personality Inventory). While not foolproof, it is remarkably good at finding dishonesty and identifying the more serious personality quirks. Urge your church to make use of such a tool. When used for everyone—even volunteers—no one feels singled out or discriminated against. Another safeguard before hiring a new staff person is to check with your police department to see if he or she has a criminal record.

2. *Closely supervise staff and volunteers.* Periodically give children, youth, and parents questionnaires to fill out about the church staff and programs. Carefully avoid creating a climate of suspicion or undermining; simply look for constructive ways to improve programs and encourage leaders. Such questionnaires may help uncover problem people so they can be

helped or placed in better spots. A church Personnel Committee can offer similar oversight and support to the staff.

3. Develop educational programs for families. One church I know has a regularly repeated series of classes on Christian parenting. The staff teaches parents how to discipline their children without abusing them, and also helps parents recognize ways they may be abusing their children without realizing it. I've spent many precious hours participating in such programs.

The community in which I live has a regular set of battles about who should be teaching sex education. Parents feel the schools' perspective is too secular and liberal. Schools counter by saying, "If you don't like the job we're doing, then you'd better start doing it yourself—because someone has to." The church carefully stays out of the fray, doing little or nothing. One very liberal church staff, however, invited me to consult with them about offering a sex education program for their youth. I was sadly disappointed to hear several members of the committee argue that "free" sex was part of adolescence and kids should be allowed and even encouraged to experiment sexually in order to learn about it.

Research done by Search Institute, Minneapolis, Minnesota, agrees with most of us in saying that church congregations have the potential to help kids develop in positive ways. But their study of 2,400 youth in five mainline Protestant denominations revealed that:

- Only 43 percent report real care from adults in their churches.
- Only 40 percent said their churches did a good job of helping them serve other people.
- A startling 74 percent are involved in one or more of

ten risky behaviors (drugs, sex, drinking, etc.), and 31 percent were involved in three or more.
- Only 51 percent of church youth said their congregation does a good job of giving them a sense of purpose in life.[1]

4. Organize adult prayer partners to meet with each other and with kids. Yes, this involves some risk. Gossip about private concerns can get out. A bad adult-child match could occur. Yet the good mentoring and immeasurable power of prayer surely are worth those risks. What security it provides for children to know they are important enough for someone to promise to pray regularly for them!

5. Develop resources. Churches need to collect books, tapes, and videos that teach good parenting skills. They need to provide information to their members about abuse: the forms it can take, how to prevent it, how to help children recognize it and avoid becoming either victims or abusers. Young people can be unbelievably abusive, verbally and even physically, to parents and teachers as well as to one other.

The church must also assume some responsibility for encouraging a wholesome lifestyle, including warning families about the potential dangers of the media and the Internet. One need not be a calamity howler to face the truth about the deterioration of TV programs. The series that airs "funny" home videos now shows clips in which danger or actual harm to children is portrayed as comical. Violence, victimization, and sexually explicit scenes are regular fare on prime-time TV. The climate created by these programs robs children of their innocence and opens doors wide to adolescent experimentation. Encouraging abusive behavior is abuse!

What One Church Did

Many years ago I spoke in a church that had truly developed a vision for itself as an active, compassionate member of the community. The leaders and members chose to abuse-proof the children in the church by addressing the needs of the parents. Here's what they did:

- Found and developed inexpensive housing for single moms. They matched a mentor family to each single-parent family to offer support and relief for the mom and help and encouragement for the kids. They developed a job register and taught home and financial management to the overstressed single parents.
- Organized an after-school program for the children of these and other single-parent families. They loved them, fed them, taught them to play, and helped them with their homework. They met and encouraged the parents, often discovering special needs the church could help to meet.
- Encouraged these single parents to join Bible studies and other interest groups and provided child care and household help so the parents could attend. This helped relieve the loneliness so common among abusive parents.
- Offered loveliness to deprived families who otherwise knew barren surroundings. They set up a clothes closet complete with hair care and cosmetics so the single moms could look nice. They found decorations and decent furnishings for their apartments.
- Often provided a used car to aid a family in multiple ways.

You, too, can organize and facilitate a widespread transformation in your community. It takes vision, self-sacrifice, volunteers, some organization and planning, and lots of donations. Think about what you and your church could do to transform your neighborhood—and in the process nearly eliminate child abuse in your small part of the world. Perhaps your vision will spread.

The church has many wonderful opportunities to help prevent child abuse. And remember—*you* are the church.

9

Finding Healing and Forgiveness

Sadness flooded six-year-old Arden's face. His obviously angry father and worried, tender mother sat on either side of him, telling me his tragic story of lost innocence.

The fourteen-year-old son of some church friends had offered to entertain Arden so the parents could talk together after a family dinner. On their way home that evening, Arden fell asleep, but the next day he was a different child than he had been. Usually energetic and bubbling with the joy of living, Arden woke up tense and irritable, and he avoided his family. When a time-out and scolding failed to restore his good nature, Arden's mother took him to her room, held him firmly yet lovingly, and asked, "What is wrong? You have never acted like this before."

After a few minutes of tense silence, out came the sordid details of what Arden's "playmate" had done to him the night before. He really didn't have all the words with which to describe the sexual abuse, but his mother got the picture, clear and ugly. Her effervescent son had been robbed of his innocence, exploited like a toy for the teen's excitement.

The family came to me, wanting to know what to do. With every fiber of his being, Dad wanted to retaliate, to hit and yell, to attack both the teen and his parents. Mom felt like cheering Dad on in such an assault. Fortunately, they waited to do anything until they regained control of their feelings.

In working with this family and others in similar circumstances, my first concern is for the victim, and then with stopping the perpetrator. Arden's parents had been close friends of the family of the teenager, and would not reveal their identity. All I could do was inform them of the law and ask them to report this tragic event to help prevent the same thing from happening to other children. I then focused on helping Arden recover.

Helping Your Child Heal

To help your child heal from an abusive episode, remember the following:

1. Every sexual abuse victim needs to hear words such as these from his or her parents:

- We will never let you suffer such abuse again. As far as we are able, we will protect you. But you must be responsible to run to us, or to a safe adult like a teacher, if anyone ever tries to use bad touch with you.
- It was wrong for Harold to touch your private parts, but you did nothing wrong.
- You must never touch anyone else the way he touched you.
- Let me repeat, if anyone else ever tries to do anything like that to you again, you must run away and tell us all about it. This is not tattling.
- What Harold did to you is against the law and has to be reported to the child welfare people. That, too, is not your fault. Reporting it is important because it may stop Harold from ever doing this to another child.

- Whenever you feel sad, angry, or scared about this event, talk to us about your feelings.
- As time goes by, you will mostly forget about this, and we will let you forget it.
- Ask God to comfort you, to heal Harold, and to help you be able to forgive him.

2. Balance the attention you give to the victim—not too much and not too little. In an effort to assure that a victim does not carry ugly scars for a lifetime, both counselors and parents may talk too much, ask too many questions, and actually prolong the pain unnecessarily. This is particularly true for sexual abuse.

3. Try to be genuine about your own feelings while remaining controlled as you express them. Encourage your child to share feelings as openly as he or she can. Your child may be angry, sad, fearful, or even feel a wish for revenge. Whatever the emotions, they are real, and real feelings are okay. The more they are talked or cried out, the less likely the child will be to act them out. Encourage any victimized child to get out his or her thoughts and feelings rather than act on them.

4. For complete healing, your child needs to forgive—a difficult process that may take some time. In general, however, children are by nature ready to forgive and move on with their activities. Adults must allow them to do so, even when the adults themselves are not so quick to let go. So keep striving to get at the child's feelings, identify them, express them, and then get on with the healing.

Your child may very well need the help of a therapist who specializes in children and abuse. Choose such help carefully. Look for someone who understands the dynamics of family interactions. No one in a family suffers alone, and everyone must also be involved in the healing process.

While these principles are specifically geared to helping children heal from sexual abuse, many children also need healing from the physical abuse that comes with overly harsh punishment. From 1986 to 1993, the total number of children who suffered abuse and neglect doubled, and the number of children seriously injured quadrupled.[1] We must stop this exponential growth in damage to our children. And each of you who reads this book can help.

Let me remind you of a fact you probably know: scars result from injuries to the skin. And scar tissue is tough.

Emotional wounds leave scars, too. We all wish our children could escape without scars when they suffer abuse, but that's not always possible. Once an injury occurs, the best we can do for a child—and this is not a small thing—is to help that child see the scar as evidence that he or she survived massive trauma with courage and wisdom.

Healing for Adult Victims

Adult victims of childhood abuse are much more difficult to treat than children. For one thing, many have tried so hard to forget their abuse that they become confused about what really happened. They may have major problems in their social lives, and marital sexual adjustments may be a source of great difficulty. One authority says that some two-thirds of sexually abused children who show symptoms as a result of the abuse recover significantly during the first year or eighteen months after the abuse. About one-third of sexual abuse victims do not show symptoms at the time; we do, however, sometimes see these symptoms emerge later, as when marital sex recalls old injuries.[2]

It has been my experience that adult victims of childhood

sexual abuse can come to healing through telling their sad, painful story to someone they trust—just as talking and expressing their feelings can help children heal. The one significant difference in an adult's ability to heal lies in the area of guilt feelings. Over time, repeatedly molested children experience sexual excitement that may or may not be pleasurable, and they begin to assume some responsibility for the encounters. Nearly always, they then feel great remorse and guilt. They experience an intense emotional tug-of-war. Part of them can enjoy the sexual feelings, but a different part dreads, hates, and feels guilty about it. In later life, these conflicts create intense anxiety and depression. Let me add that I have worked with some children who share these feelings with adults.

Good psychotherapy is immensely helpful for such distressed adults, promoting healing by helping the victim:

- Discover who was really guilty for the abuse.
- Understand why the abuser did what he did and eventually forgive him.
- Release his own guilt.
- Resist the temptation either to repeat the abuse or to excuse it.

Sometimes I think parents of abused children suffer even more than their child does. Whether their guilt comes from not having been able to protect their child or from having lost control and abusing the child themselves, it can feel unbearable.

If you have abused your child, you must learn to forgive yourself. You must ask God to forgive you. You must ask your child to forgive you. And above all, you must stop your abusive actions and never again do any abusive thing. Get help. Go back to chapter 2 for a list of resources.

But How Can I Ever Forgive?

Today a friend, Lucy, told me this tragic, transgenerational story. She is seeking a divorce and has moved out of a lovely home into a small apartment with her six-year-old son, who is grieving over the loss of his home and the daddy he loves. He is bewildered and torn by his parents' fighting and separation.

Lucy's husband, Stan, is the grandson of an alcoholic who made life miserable for his family. Stan's father was a controlling, almost tyrannical father. Alcoholism creates chaos in many families, and children discover early that some order can be found if they keep everything under control. These children survive by learning how to control their world.

Stan learned from his obsessive father how to keep a family structured. In his marriage to Lucy, he managed the money, made most of the decisions, and kept a tight rein on everything.

Lucy grew up in a family where her parents argued excessively. They did not trust each other, and finally Dad moved out. Their divorce made Lucy's life very difficult, and she recalls feeling confused, helpless, and angry with both her parents.

At first Lucy loved having Stan make the decisions and manage their lives, but when their baby was born, she realized that she had to be mature enough to parent their son. Lucy now wanted to make some decisions on her own. She needed to understand their financial situation, and she sorely needed a husband who wanted to be a good father.

The birth of their child was the point at which Stan and Lucy's troubles erupted. They'd been brewing for generations, but now they exploded. Unable to cope with all the changes in his life, Stan escaped through TV and sports, leaving Lucy to deal with the baby all alone. He not only neglected his wife and son, but verbally abused them. The pain of it all became overwhelming for Lucy, and she finally found peace through separation.

What a lot of heartache could have been prevented had both Lucy's and Stan's parents practiced forgiveness instead of codependency. Stan's dad could have given up his need for control, and with a different model to emulate, Stan would have been able to share the running of his and Lucy's home with her. She would never have had to endure his abuse because he'd never have done it. And had Lucy's mom and dad learned to love and trust each other, their divorce would not have taken place. Lucy could have developed into a mature woman before her marriage and been a true partner from the beginning of her relationship with Stan.

Forgiving—A Process

I used to view forgiveness as a glib, impulsive action that we needed to do in order to avoid guilt and to be obedient to biblical commands. Through my own storms and struggles, I've learned that forgiveness is not a one-time event, nor does it happen overnight.

The following steps are part of the forgiveness process:

1. We must be ready to forgive. Lucy is so wounded that she flinches when her phone rings. Stan is abusive in his efforts to get her back and is unwittingly driving her farther away. She can't even imagine forgiving the man she now sees as a brute.

2. We must acknowledge our pain. It's comforting to say to ourselves, "He can't hurt me. He's such a louse, I don't care what he does!" It sounds tough and self-protective, but Stan still can and does hurt Lucy, even though they're separated.

When we say to anyone, "I love you," we give that person the power to hurt us. But we need never—we *must* never—give anyone the power to devastate or destroy us.

3. When we recover enough from our wounds to be able to think logically, we must find out why that loved person hurt us. Much of the help and hope I offer my patients comes through helping them learn the truth. For example, Stan had no intention of abusing Lucy, much less their son. He only sensed that he desperately needed control so that he (and the family as he saw it) could feel safe. He had always lived with and practiced immense control. He felt he was being the protector of his family by being in charge.

4. We must allow the facts we discover to bring insight. Insight is the priceless gift that allows knowledge to create understanding. It may be only a few inches from one's head to one's heart, but without insight, it might as well be a million miles. Sometimes we don't want insight because we know it will bring us closer to forgiveness—and we don't always want to forgive. We like staying just a little bit mad; it feels safer.

5. When understanding is complete, we enjoy what I call an "Aha!" experience. Much of the pain of abuse comes from the victim's feeling that "The abuse is my fault. I'm the problem." When understanding and insight come, the victim can see clearly, "It's not my fault! I'm not bad, and it's not my problem that this occurred. It's the problem of my offender." With this revelation, the victim is free from guilt, helplessness, and pain. As a therapist, I can see that Stan was only living out his life script, taught carefully by his father, who learned it from his grandfather. He never intended to be selfish or abusive—only safe. If only Lucy could have understood that, she might have been free of her pain, free to take the next step, forgiveness.

6. Forgiving is the joy of accepting the "Aha!" experience and choosing to relinquish our self-pity and pain (often the result of misunderstanding). Interestingly, the freedom we experience when we relinquish our pain and self-pity can so change us that our abusers finally see their errors and change for the better. There's no guarantee of that happening, for sure, but when we are free of hurt, when we lose our wish to retaliate and find a brand-new, healthy lifestyle, we are certainly winners.[3]

Some people seem to think that forgiving someone who has wronged them means condoning the abusive behavior and excusing the abuser. Nothing could be further from the truth. You can both forgive and set clear boundaries to protect yourself from further abuse from that person.

Setting Boundaries With the Offender

If Lucy would let me, here's what I'd tell her about how to set limits with Stan:

First, Lucy needs to get clear in her own mind just what areas of family management will be under her jurisdiction. She might choose menu-planning and interior decorating. She'd seek Stan's ideas and consider his preferences, but those areas would be hers. Stan might manage the vehicles and the lawn. Together they might handle the chores and the family finances. Of course, they might choose other divisions of labor, and they would always consult with and inform each other.

Next, Lucy would find a time when both she and Stan were calm and reasonable and present her plan to him, explaining her ideas. She would invite Stan's input and negotiate a trial plan with him. She would keep an open mind and be willing to make changes as needed.

If Stan reverted to his domineering ways, Lucy would clearly, but kindly, point that out. She would remind him of their agreement and tell him she was going out for a thirty-minute walk while he thought about things and watched their son, Jed. After her walk, Lucy would return home calm and ready to resume problem-solving, but she wouldn't fight, argue, or get into a no-win power struggle. Lucy might have to wait some days for Stan to "get it," but she wouldn't give in and break their agreement. What a nice way to manage a family!

Helping Children Set Boundaries

Children are role models for forgiving. Perhaps out of their need and the very fact of their vulnerability, they quickly get emotional but equally soon they reason things out and get on with their play, tasks, or whatever.

A bit of parental supervision and guidance can teach cooperation and problem-solving between siblings and restore harmony in the household. Yet kids may have a more difficult time setting boundaries with the occasional teacher, bully, or abusive parent. My son, Lyndon, had a truly abusive guitar teacher when he was only twelve. The man was so rude I wanted to tell him off! "Mom, will you let me handle it?" he asked.

Upset as I was, I decided that maybe he could handle the situation better than I could. And he did. He calmly told his teacher that he did not do well with angry lectures. He was willing to work and he wanted to learn, but the teacher's angry words only made him feel tense and awkward. To my astonishment, the man listened to my very wise son and mellowed his behavior.

My husband was more strict than I was in his correction of our three kids, and at times became angry with them. For some years I ran interference and tried to smooth things out for everyone. I realized at last how wrong I was, and explained to the children that I would no longer be their go-between with Dad. I helped them learn how to say, for example, "Dad, when you yell at me, it scares me. I don't like being scared of you!" He didn't like for them to be scared either, so he learned to correct them more gently.

Children not only can forgive abuse, they can also set boundaries that help protect them from further maltreatment. All they need is an adult to teach them how—or even to give them the green light to set their own limits.

You may need to forgive your parents or even your grandparents. You may need to forgive friends, relatives, your spouse, or your children. Hardest of all, you may have to admit your own wrongdoing and forgive yourself. Please do so as soon as you are ready to do it honestly. When you have learned the process and practiced it consistently, teach these steps to your children.

Forgiveness is the way to real freedom, strength, and great joy. It is as fulfilling once completed as it seems difficult beforehand.

Whether abuse has been physical, emotional, sexual, or maltreatment by neglect, you can forgive your offender. And you must teach your child to forgive his or her offender as well.

Start Today

If you have read this book, it's likely that you want to be a parent who does all that you can to protect and nurture your child. My prayer is that the Holy Spirit will use the information you've received to guide you toward changes you may need to make in order to abuse-proof your children. For some of you, this may mean getting counseling or confronting people you love about their actions. This is tough stuff, but you must do what you can to protect your child from abuse. Remember, when it comes to abuse-proofing your kids, *you* are the most important key. Start today!

Notes

ONE
Recognizing Child Abuse

1. Grace Ketterman, *You & Your Child's Problems* (Old Tappan, N.J.: Revell, 1983), 353.
2. David Wolfe, *Child Abuse*, 2d ed. (Thousand Oaks, Calif.: Sage Publications, 1999), 11.
3. C.T. Wang and D. Daro, *Current Trends in Child Abuse Reporting and Fatalities: The Results of the 1997 Annual Fifty State Survey* (Chicago: Prevent Child Abuse America, 1998).
4. Jim Hopper, "Child Abuse: Statistics, Research, & Resources," cited 24 July 1998 at http://www.jimhopper.com/abstats/INTERNET.

TWO
Is Your Child Safe With YOU?

1. Wang and Daro.
2. See Grace Ketterman and Pat Holt, *When You Feel Like Screaming* (Wheaton, Ill.: Harold Shaw, 1988).
3. Wolfe, 76.

4. U.S. Census Bureau, quoted by Bill O'Reilly, *Parade Magazine,* 26 March 2000, 5.
5. See Grace Ketterman, *Verbal Abuse* (Ann Arbor, Mich.: Servant, 1992).

FIVE

Passing on Healthy Attitudes About Sex

1. Jennifer Freyd, as quoted in Hopper.

SIX

Is Your Child Safe at Home and at Play?

1. Wolfe, 31.

EIGHT

Is Your Child Safe at Church?

1. Peter Benson and Eugene C. Roehlkepartain, "Congregations as Partners in Positive Youth Development," *Source* (Minneapolis: Search Institute, 1994), 2.

NINE

Finding Healing and Forgiveness

1. Wolfe, 10ff.

2. Wolfe, 10ff.
3. See Grace Ketterman and David Hazard, *When You Can't Say "I Forgive You"* (Colorado Springs: NavPress, 2000).